Up to Jerusalem

Devotions for Lent and Easter

John A. Braun

NORTHWESTERN PUBLISHING HOUSE
Milwaukee, Wisconsin

D1411402

Second printing, 1998

Library of Congress Card 97-69278
Northwestern Publishing House
1250 N. 113th St., Milwaukee, WI 53226-3284
© 1997 by Northwestern Publishing House.
Published 1997
Printed in the United States of America
ISBN 0-8100-0795-9

Contents

Foreword

Let's walk with Jesus!

Let's go up to Jerusalem with Jesus on his last trip. For him it was a trip to the cross. For us it is a spiritual trip, a pilgrimage to think again about what Jesus did for us.

As a disciple of Jesus, my world is different from the world of those first disciples. I do not walk along dusty roads to follow Jesus or sit in the hot sun to listen to his words. But I am a disciple of Jesus. He has called me to be his disciple as clearly and certainly as he called Matthew from his tax booth or Peter, James, and John from their fishing nets and boats. I follow Jesus because he loves me and died for me. Like those first disciples, I listen to his words, but now I sit quietly and listen to or read his inspired written Word.

Jesus has called millions of disciples over the centuries. Each of those disciples has been drawn to Jerusalem and the cross. Over the centuries believers have traveled up to Jerusalem to visit the places where the Savior of the world suffered and died. Some have actually made the journey to stand and walk in Jerusalem. But most of us have not been able to be in Jerusalem or stand at the Mount of Olives. Instead, we have made regular spiritual journeys to Jerusalem. Each time we read of the Savior's final journey, we travel with him in spirit. Most often we use the season of Lent to make our annual spiritual journey up to Jerusalem. I have taken that journey regularly as I listen to the reading of the passion history, sing the Lenten hymns, and meditate on my sins and God's grace in sending Jesus.

These devotions are the result of my spiritual journeys up to Jerusalem with Jesus. I invite you to travel with me to meditate on the love of Jesus for us. The devotions trace the Savior's steps to the cross and the grave. I have chosen to start with the raising of Lazarus, the miracle that convinced the Jewish leaders that Jesus had to die.

You should understand that in some cases we do not know the exact details of these events. Wherever there may be a difference of opinion on the sequence of events, I have chosen one approach over another. I do understand that there are other opinions about the chronology, geography, and other details. Thousands of pages have been written about those differences. For these devotions, however, I'm more interested in the events themselves than the speculation. These events did take place. Of that there is no question. I trust the Bible's record because it is God's inspired record and gives me all I need to know for my salvation. God left no doubt that Jesus shed his blood for the sins of the world and rose again, leaving his tomb empty.

So come and go up to Jerusalem again. I hope you will take the journey often. I have always found something new to learn or something I have forgotten. As you walk with Jesus, he will strengthen your faith and prepare you for your journey ahead.

1

Resurrection and Life

Jesus, once more deeply moved, came to the tomb. It was a cave with a stone laid across the entrance. "Take away the stone," he said. "But, Lord," said Martha, the sister of the dead man, "by this time there is a bad odor, for he has been there four days." So they took away the stone. . . . Jesus called in a loud voice, "Lazarus, come out!" The dead man came out, his hands and feet wrapped with strips of linen, and a cloth around his face. Jesus said to them, "Take off the grave clothes and let him go." (John 11:38,39,41,43,44)

When Jesus heard that his friend Lazarus was sick, he waited two days before going to Bethany. When the message about his friend came, he was across the Jordan River, in the area where John the Baptist had been baptizing about three years earlier. Jesus went there because the Jews had tried to arrest him the last time he was in Jerusalem. He was safe in Perea, just far enough away from the Jewish high council, the Sanhedrin, in Jerusalem. Many ordinary people, however, came to him there as they had come to hear John. When they heard Jesus, many believed that Jesus was the Messiah John had announced. But the news from Mary and Martha interrupted Jesus' work.

The walk from Perea to Bethany took two days. Jesus and his disciples walked along the road that crossed the Jordan and went through Jericho. From the river the road slowly rose as it approached Jerusalem. Bethany was less than two miles from the Holy City. Jesus had visited the house of Mary and Martha many times before. The welcome was always overwhelming. Martha made sure that Jesus and the others had enough food to eat, and Mary longed for each word that Jesus spoke as she sat attentively at his feet.

The day Jesus arrived this time was a day of sorrow. Lazarus, the brother of Mary and Martha, was dead. While Jesus was still a long way off, Martha ran toward him. In her grief she told Jesus that if he had been there, her brother would not have died. Jesus reassured her by promising that her brother would rise again. Martha trusted that Lazarus would rise again at the Last Day, but Jesus reminded her: "I am the resurrection and the life. He who believes in me will live, even though he dies; and whoever lives and believes in me will never die" (John 11:25,26). Then Martha went back to Bethany to tell Mary that Jesus had arrived.

Mary came quickly to Jesus. She was weeping as she fell at his feet and poured out her heart in almost the same words her sister had used. Jesus was deeply moved, and tears formed at the corners of his eyes and wetted his cheeks on their way to his beard. As Jesus approached the tomb of Lazarus, he might have wiped the tears from his face with the tips of his fingers. It was four days since Lazarus had died.

What happened next can never be forgotten. With a voice so loud that it seemed everyone in Bethany and maybe even in Jerusalem could hear him, Jesus called, "Lazarus, come out!" The dead man obeyed!

If this was a trip to the stronghold of Jesus' enemies in Judea, they could not put him to death. Instead, Jesus brought life and resurrection—joy and hope. What a way to start this final walk with Jesus! If we had been there, we would have talked for days about how we saw Lazarus stand at the dark entrance of his tomb still wrapped in the strips of linen used to bury him. Jesus had called him back to life.

The words of comfort Jesus spoke to Mary about being the resurrection and the life powerfully and dramatically became more than just words. They were true because Jesus stood behind them. For him the death of Lazarus was no more than a sleep from which he could awaken his friend. The loud voice of Jesus at the tomb and the miracle brought tears of joy and astonishment to everyone there. I have come to treasure the concept of death as a sleep from which my great friend, Jesus, will awaken me too.

The powerful voice of Jesus did echo in Jerusalem, a couple miles away. Reports of the miracle came to the Pharisees, who quickly called a meeting of the Sanhedrin. The Jewish high council resolved to kill Jesus because he was performing too many miraculous signs. Isn't it strange that such life-giving power should create a desire for death?

In that special meeting of the Jewish council, Caiaphas, the high priest, said, "You do not realize that it is better for you that one man die for the people than that the whole nation perish" (John 11:50). He was willing to sacrifice Jesus so that he and the others could continue as the leaders of the Jews. The enemies of Jesus reasoned that his growing popularity would take people away from the Jewish traditions and temple.

Ironically, what Caiaphas meant was not what God meant. God's long-awaited plan was about to unfold. One man would die for the people so that the whole nation would not perish. Jesus would die so that every Jew and every Gentile would not perish but have eternal life. From the death of Jesus would come life and resurrection. That was something Caiaphas could not understand. He was blinded by unbelief.

PRAYER: As I begin this journey with you, Lord Jesus, open my eyes to see your power over death. Open my heart to treasure the greatness of your love for all of us mortal creatures. Open my mind to see your great plan to die for me and for all the world so we might live. Thank you, Lord, for your tears; each one reminds me that you love your friends deeply and care about their pain and sorrow. Pour the healing comfort of your Word into the wounds of my soul so that I may follow along the path you trace for me. Amen.

2

Morning Devotion

So from that day on they plotted to take his life. Therefore Jesus no longer moved about publicly among the Jews. Instead he withdrew to a region near the desert, to a village called Ephraim, where he stayed with his disciples. (John 11:53,54)

After the raising of Lazarus, the Jewish leaders became as hard as stone. One thing had to happen to Jesus: he must die. But the time had not yet come for Jesus to die. Jesus withdrew to a small village called Ephraim with his disciples. There he would quietly teach them for a few more days, away from the swarming dust and noise of the crowds. For a few more days he stayed far away from the threat of the Sanhedrin. While the disciples were with Jesus in Ephraim, they sat and listened attentively again to Jesus' words. They were strengthened by the resurrection of Lazarus and the words of Jesus.

We don't know for sure where this little village was. It doesn't matter. Jesus knew, and he went there to wait for the Passover. His time was coming. He knew it clearly. He knew every detail of his final journey to Jerusalem and the final Passover, but he waited and taught his disciples. The disciples must have sensed that something great and important was about to happen. They knew the Jewish leaders wanted Jesus dead; they feared they too would die. Each morning the sun rose, and the disciples would once again sit at the feet of Jesus. Jerusalem boiled with opposition miles away. But in this little village, the sunrise reminded the disciples of the beauty of God's creation. Yes, "the heavens declare the glory of God; the skies proclaim the work of his hands" (Psalm 19:1).

I'm always fascinated by the morning and sunrise. God colors the sky with so much beauty every morning. At first the morning is quiet and dark, and then long before the sun rises, the birds begin to sing. I always get a sense of peace and eagerness for the events of a new day. The air is still and cool as the sky in the east changes from the cold, dark gray to the lighter gray of predawn. From the lighter grays, gradually a purple then a dusty red emerge, each in its turn.

Some of the night stars still burn in the changing sky, but they slowly disappear. Sometimes the morning star stays long after the other stars have retreated, as if it were the rear guard for the thousands that had disappeared. If the moon has risen late, it stays too, fading as the sky brightens.

When the sun begins to rise in the far horizon, its first arc appears. In Ephraim it must have looked like the leading edge of a giant, glowing red ball pushing itself up from beneath the sand-covered horizon. The more that red ball pushes upward toward the sky, the brighter it becomes, changing from red to orange and finally to bright yellow. The shift from gray to yellow is a gradual one, but it never takes very long. If you don't stop to watch it, you only realize the sun is up because the first warming rays of the sun caress you after a cold damp night.

When I see the sunrise, I always feel so small and insignificant. It's as if I am standing alone before the great power and majesty of God. Part of me is filled with awe and wonder at what I see. Then when the light of the sun brightens and the beauty of the sunrise evaporates with the morning dew, I sense my own unworthiness. Inside myself I find sin. Although I often resolve to praise God for his goodness to me and all the world, only a few hours later I find I have cursed someone, shown anger, and revealed the harsh, cruel, and bitter side within. I am a sinner. I do not deserve any of what I see in the morning sky. God should punish me and everyone who lives under the sun.

I know that the psalmist who found the glory of God in the heavens also found a more important light—God's Word. That light chased away the darkness of sin within. It gave light to the psalmist's eyes, created joy in his heart, and revived his soul. What he found in God's Word was God's radiant light of forgiveness. Within his sinful and perverse heart, God's Word rose like the sun and brought peace and beauty. As for the psalmist, God's loving-kindness for me, an unworthy sinner, has arisen too. Whether I'm in a quiet little place like Ephraim or in the hard streets of the city, God loves me and forgives me. I have to pray with the psalmist every day, "Forgive my hidden faults" (Psalm 19:12), because the darkness of sin encroaches on the light of forgiveness.

That's also why I'm following Jesus. Those of us who have become his followers know our sinfulness—our unworthiness before the great power and majesty of a holy God. Yet in Jesus we find God's grace. He gently blessed the children, tenderly understood the problems of those who came to him, and compassionately healed those with diseases. He hasn't changed. He still delicately touches us all with the words he spoke and caused to be written. He is the great sunrise of God in this darkness of sin and death. The resurrection of Lazarus assured that to all Jesus' disciples of all time.

We follow Jesus because we want the warmth and light he brings. Is there any wonder that we eagerly listen when he teaches? Sometimes we find a quiet place to read his Word. We also go to his house, where we can shut out the noise of everyday life and pause with our fellow disciples to listen to Jesus. Away from his Word, the darkness continues to spread. If we don't listen to Jesus, the noise and darkness will rob us of our light.

PRAYER: The heavens declare the glory of God; the skies proclaim the work of his hands. . . . Forgive my hidden faults. Keep your servant also from willful sins; may they not rule over me. Then will I be blameless, innocent of great transgression. May the words of my mouth and the meditation of my heart be pleasing in your sight, O LORD, my Rock and my Redeemer (Psalm 19:1,12-14). Amen.

3

To Jerusalem to Die

Jesus took the Twelve aside and told them, "We are going up to Jerusalem, and everything that is written by the prophets about the Son of Man will be fulfilled. He will be handed over to the Gentiles. They will mock him, insult him, spit on him, flog him and kill him. On the third day he will rise again." The disciples did not understand any of this. Its meaning was hidden from them, and they did not know what he was talking about. (Luke 18:31-34)

When God called Gideon so long ago to fight against the overwhelming army of the Midianites, the Angel of the Lord addressed him, "The LORD is with you, mighty warrior" (Judges 6:12). Those words are worth remembering when we think of Jesus and his disciples. For Jesus is another mighty warrior who we know has battled sin, death, and hell in order to save us.

When Jesus and his disciples arrived in Ephraim (John 11:54), the Passover was only a couple weeks away. The chief priests and Pharisees had ordered everyone to tell them where Jesus was so they could arrest him. But no one came to arrest him in Ephraim. When it was time for the Passover, Jesus led the way to Jerusalem. With his disciples Jesus traveled toward the Jordan River, where they would join the many pilgrims on the road from Galilee. No doubt Peter and the other apostles were astonished at the resolve of Jesus to go to Jerusalem. They all knew it was a journey to death; Jesus had clearly told them so.

The roads to Jerusalem were always busy at the time of the Passover. Thousands walked to Jerusalem to observe the Passover. Jesus and the disciples had traveled the roads many times before. When they reached the Jordan River, they must have met many people from Galilee. Because Jesus had spent most of his ministry in

Galilee, the people knew Jesus well. Along the way the disciples must have talked to people they had not seen in months. Perhaps they shared news of what Jesus had done in Bethany. Or maybe they still talked of the miracles Jesus had performed in Galilee, especially the great feeding at the Sea of Galilee. Like all pilgrims on the way to the Holy City, they sang the psalms of ascent (Psalms 120–134) as they walked with Jesus and prepared themselves for the great festival of Passover.

As clear as Jesus had been about the purpose for this final trip, the disciples still did not understand it. Why did Jesus head toward Jerusalem? Do we understand? Jesus could have stayed in Ephraim, just out of his enemies' reach. Was he drawn to Jerusalem as a moth is drawn to the fatal flame? Was he helpless in the face of political intrigue and resolute opposition?

Jesus was not helpless. He had raised Lazarus from the dead. He had fed the multitudes. He had healed the sick and lame. He had made fevers vanish with a word. Jesus went to Jerusalem willingly, knowing exactly what would happen. He went because he loved me and all the world. Had he hid in Ephraim or disappeared among the crowds, I would have no forgiveness before God and no hope of life in heaven. Because he went to Jerusalem, I am forgiven, washed by his blood, and I live in the hope of the resurrection and life eternal. So do all who follow Jesus.

Jesus and his disciples mingled with the crowd on the road to Jerusalem. Little did anyone know then that Jesus was going to Jerusalem to offer himself as the sacrificial Passover lamb. How dense they all were! Even the closest disciples failed to grasp the significance of walking alongside the Lamb of God to his sacrificial death for the sins of the world. All these things were hidden from them at the time. They could have remembered what John the Baptist had said. Three years earlier, at the Jordan River, John had pointed to Jesus and said, "Look, the Lamb of God, who takes away the sin of the world!" (John 1:29). But they didn't remember until it was all over.

Then the disciples understood that Jesus was the one great Passover Lamb to whom all the other lambs pointed. His blood was shed to save them and the entire world from death and God's punishment, just as the blood of the lambs splashed on the doorposts had saved the Israelites in Egypt. All the Old Testament Scriptures pointed to this final trip to Jerusalem, where Jesus, the Lamb of God, would die and rise again.

Even though the disciples did not understand at the time, Jesus was determined about going to Jerusalem because he was ready to complete God's plan of salvation. His hour had come. He would not hide from the anger and venom of the chief priests and Pharisees any longer. Jesus showed more than just resignation in his steps. He advanced to Jerusalem willingly because he loved us all very much. Yes, we learn how Jesus showed the full extent of his love as he resolutely did what he had to do to bring us forgiveness and eternal life (John 13:1).

Gideon was a mighty warrior, but Jesus displayed more valor by lovingly and courageously walking toward Jerusalem knowing exactly what would happen.

———

PRAYER: Lamb of God, pure and holy, who on the cross did suffer, ever patient and lowly, yourself to scorn did offer. All sins you carried for us, else had despair reigned over us: Have mercy on us, O Jesus! (CW 268:1).

———

4

Vision in Jericho

As Jesus and his disciples were leaving Jericho, a large crowd followed him. Two blind men were sitting by the roadside, and when they heard that Jesus was going by, they shouted, "Lord, Son of David, have mercy on us!" The crowd rebuked them and told them to be quiet, but they shouted all the louder, "Lord, Son of David, have mercy on us!" Jesus stopped and called them. "What do you want me to do for you?" he asked. "Lord," they answered, "we want our sight." Jesus had compassion on them and touched their eyes. Immediately they received their sight and followed him. (Matthew 20:29-34)

The last major city on the road to Jerusalem was Jericho, an important city controlling the surrounding plains. So much had happened in this place. Over a thousand years before Jesus, Joshua and God's people had marched around old Jericho, and the walls fell down. Through the centuries the city was destroyed and rebuilt many times. After every defeat and destruction, someone rebuilt it again because of its strategic position. The Romans made it an important customs station to tax the caravans traveling along the road. Herod the Great often spent winters in Jericho because it was warmer than Caesarea. He built a theater, fortress, hippodrome, and palace there.

In Jesus' day Jericho was always busy. At Passover time it must have been especially busy, as pilgrims on their way to Jerusalem walked along with the caravans. Palm trees and sycamores invited travelers to rest in the shade. Most probably, the two blind men of our text sat in the shade. They perhaps sat cross-legged on the ground near the road so they could beg from pilgrims on their way to Jerusalem. As these two men heard the commotion and noise of the crowd approaching, they began to beg.

When they discovered that Jesus of Nazareth was walking by the wayside where they sat, they began to shout. As Jesus approached, their loud voices pleaded, "Lord, Son of David, have mercy on us!" Both blind men had certainly heard of Jesus. Stories of the great miracles he performed were common knowledge among the people. A once-in-a-lifetime opportunity walked by them on the path. This Son of David could cure them, so they shouted. Some in the crowd rebuked them and told them to be quiet. But the more the crowd tried to shush the men, the louder and more insistent the men became: "Son of David, have mercy on us!" Finally their cries pierced the noise of the crowd and brought the procession to a halt. Their cries for help stopped Jesus.

What a wonderful thought! Jesus stopped because someone needed help. He was headed for Jerusalem, but he was not too busy to help two blind beggars along the road. How often I have felt like a poor beggar. Sometimes life overwhelms me. Sometimes I seem to be a spectator watching the world go by. I wonder whether I can fit into the procession. At other times I feel helpless, guilty, frustrated, lonely, and desperate. My opportunity for help comes too. Jesus is always as close as my cry for mercy. So I pray!

Jesus stopped to help. Two blind men received their sight. The miracle again confirmed the power of Jesus. Just think: Jesus said a word to a couple blind men, and their eyes could see. No one could do that but God himself. No doctor could heal with a word. But Jesus did it, because he is the Son of God. If he can command blindness away, every word he says has power. So I trust that Jesus will stop to help me too and answer my cry for mercy. I may endure gloomy troubles and dark woes, but Jesus will stop when I pray.

When Jesus answers our prayers, he often gives us more than we ask. These men asked to see. When their eyes focused on the shapes in the light, they saw Jesus. They joyfully followed him from that day on. Remember where Jesus was going? Jerusalem was only about 17 miles away, and the Passover was about a week away. Both men followed Jesus all the way to Jerusalem. During those first days of new vision, not only did they see the sunshine, trees, people, and cities of Judea, but they also saw Jesus on the way to Jerusalem to suffer and die and rise again for them as their Savior.

The Son of David came into the dark world of the two blind men and gave them light beyond their expectations. They only had wanted to see, and Jesus opened their eyes in time so that they could see what all God's people throughout history longed to see. David himself and all the believers of old longed to see Jesus accomplish the salvation of the world. We and thousands like us, born after these events, can never see these things with our own eyes. We must rely on the vision of faith. By faith we can see Jesus suffering and dying for our sins. By faith we can see the empty tomb, which proclaims God's verdict of justification to the world.

PRAYER: Son of David, do not pass by without stopping today. I am in need of mercy. Sometimes all I see are my own daily problems. At times I can see no comfort in my difficulties and no help for my troubles. Lord, grant me sight! Open my eyes to see you standing ready to help. Open my eyes to see that you are always ready to pause and answer my prayers. Son of David, have mercy upon me. Amen.

5

Today Salvation Has Come

Jesus entered Jericho and was passing through. A man was there by the name of Zacchaeus; he was a chief tax collector and was wealthy. He wanted to see who Jesus was, but being a short man he could not, because of the crowd. So he ran ahead and climbed a sycamore-fig tree to see him, since Jesus was coming that way. When Jesus reached the spot, he looked up and said to him, "Zacchaeus, come down immediately. I must stay at your house today." So he came down at once and welcomed him gladly. (Luke 19:1-6)

As Jesus walked with his disciples toward Jericho, the news of his miraculous healing of the blind men spread quickly through the streets. Normally residents of the cities or villages in Judea welcomed pilgrims as they passed through. People often lined the streets, wishing the pilgrims a safe journey to Jerusalem and the Passover. But on this day it was different in Jericho—not that people didn't come but that the miracle brought *everyone* out to see the Son of David.

Zacchaeus heard the news too. He was a Jew and a tax collector. His Hebrew name means "pure" or "innocent," but like all tax collectors, he was far from pure. Like most tax collectors, he had cheated people by overcharging them. The Romans contracted Zacchaeus to pay them a certain amount of money, and if he collected more, he could keep it. Since the force of the Roman government was always on the side of the collector, there was little anyone could do but pay.

Jericho was in the midst of a fertile oasis; everything that was exported was taxed and every caravan that passed through the area had to pay. The Romans made Jericho an important regional customs station. The chief tax collector lived in the customhouse that the Romans built there. Under the protection of the Roman army, Zacchaeus grew wealthy.

When Zacchaeus heard that Jesus, the Son of David, was passing through Jericho on his way to Jerusalem, he knew he must see this great prophet. He ran ahead, trying to find a place from which to see Jesus, because he was too short to see over the heads of the crowd. It's not too much to imagine some of the comments that came from the crowd. Most would just as soon spit on him as talk to him.

Whatever was said, Zacchaeus was determined to see Jesus. Jericho was lined with trees. It was easy for the tax collector to run ahead of the crowd and find a sycamore-fig tree along the street where Jesus and all the others were walking. He perched himself up there in the branches of the tree and waited. I don't believe the crowd failed to notice him there or to think how much he looked like a vulture waiting for some dead carcass.

The procession slowly moved down the street to the tree where Zacchaeus held on to the branches, leaning forward to see better. Then just as Jesus had stopped for the blind men, he stopped for Zacchaeus. Jesus looked up into the branches and told Zacchaeus to come down. If Zacchaeus had been a bird, he could not have come to Jesus any more quickly.

Jesus wanted to stay at Zacchaeus' house. As soon as Jesus announced his intention, the crowd turned on him. They began to mutter, "He has gone to be the guest of a 'sinner' " (Luke 19:7)— not a pure or innocent man but a sinner who cheated them whenever he could. Nevertheless, Jesus stayed with Zacchaeus. That night Zacchaeus made a remarkable confession and pledge. Jesus had cleansed the tax collector's heart, and Zacchaeus wanted to show how he loved Jesus by doing what pleased him. He said, "Look, Lord! Here and now I give half of my possessions to the poor, and if I have cheated anybody out of anything, I will pay back four times the amount" (Luke 19:8).

Jesus said, "Today salvation has come to this house, because this man, too, is a son of Abraham. For the Son of Man came to seek and to save what was lost" (Luke 19:9,10). So many in Jericho despised Zacchaeus. He was isolated and alone. Jesus reminded him that he too was a child of God, a dear, beloved sinner whom he had come to

20

save. What a comfort to see Jesus reach out for a man whom everyone despised! The joy in Zacchaeus is also our joy, for Jesus has sought out each one of us. He has called us from our families, our friends, our businesses, our sins, our weary lives, and our fears as surely as he called Zacchaeus from the tree. Although we cannot welcome Jesus into our homes as this tax collector did, we can welcome him into our hearts and lives as Zacchaeus did.

One week before the Passover, Jesus spent the night in the home of a sinner who, having been brought to faith in Jesus, had become pure and innocent in God's sight. The blood Jesus would shed in Jerusalem cleansed Zacchaeus of his sin. It has cleansed us all so that through faith in Jesus we are forgiven, holy sons and daughters of God.

PRAYER: Lord Jesus, when all the world seems to stand against me and I appear to be an outcast, seek me out in love and remind me that you regard me as valuable and important to you. You came for me, a lost and condemned sinner. Your blood cleansed even me and made me your child. Dear Lord, when you call me to follow you, may I come to you quickly, lay aside my sins, and serve you with renewed love and devotion. Amen.

6

Preparation for Burial

Six days before the Passover, Jesus arrived at Bethany, where Lazarus lived, whom Jesus had raised from the dead. Here a dinner was given in Jesus' honor. Martha served, while Lazarus was among those reclining at the table with him. Then Mary took about a pint of pure nard, an expensive perfume; she poured it on Jesus' feet and wiped his feet with her hair. And the house was filled with the fragrance of the perfume. (John 12:1-3)

After spending the night with Zacchaeus, Jesus and his disciples resumed their journey to Jerusalem in the morning. Jerusalem was only about 17 miles away, and they intended to stop at Bethany, which was two miles from Jerusalem. The crowd that had swarmed around them as they entered Jericho gathered again with the morning light, so they all walked toward Jerusalem to celebrate the Passover. Most likely it was Friday, the day before the Sabbath.

From Jericho it was a journey up to Jerusalem. Jericho is about one thousand feet below sea level, and Jerusalem is almost three thousand feet above sea level. The road was desolate and rough—the haunt of robbers, who often attacked travelers. Jesus had made use of that fact when he told the parable of the good Samaritan.

Each step along the road brought Jesus closer to his enemies. The chief priests and Pharisees were waiting for him, but the happy spirit of the crowd must have overwhelmed any fears the disciples had. Besides, they followed Jesus. He was resolute, showing no fear of the Sanhedrin's decision to kill him. As they walked, they listened to Jesus. Whatever fears or doubts that had come into their hearts disappeared in the calm, soothing words he spoke. The two men from Jericho who had been blind also traveled with them.

Late in the afternoon they arrived at Bethany. The Sabbath came with the sunset, and Jesus intended to spend his last Sabbath with his friends. Mary, Martha, and Lazarus greeted them as they had so often before. When I think of Jesus coming to Bethany, I think what a pleasant day it must have been to come into this friendly house. As the disciples looked at Lazarus, perhaps they could still think of him standing at the entrance of his tomb, wrapped in grave clothes. The dark plot of the Jews was only two miles away, and so much was still to come. But this was a time of friendship and love.

When Jesus arrived, the family may have been putting final touches on a dinner they had planned in his honor. It was Friday, and the Sabbath began at sunset, so all the work had to be finished. Martha must have been busy preparing everything. Simon the Leper hosted the dinner at his house. Simon was one of those whom Jesus had healed long ago. His leprosy had made him an outcast and unclean, but Jesus had healed his diseased patches of skin completely. From a heart filled with gratitude, he hosted this banquet for Jesus and his disciples.

Quiet and thoughtful Mary, however, surprised everyone. While the group reclined at the table and enjoyed the dinner and conversation, Mary came up behind Jesus. She took a most beautiful smelling ointment and poured it on Jesus' feet. Everyone was stunned by Mary's action. The whole house was filled with the fragrance of the perfume. Not only did Mary pour out the perfume on Jesus' feet, but she also loosened her long hair and wiped his feet with it. A Jewish woman was not to loose her hair in the presence of men, but on that day it seemed more a tender gesture of respect and love than a breech of common courtesy and etiquette.

Only one objected—Judas Iscariot. He didn't say Mary shouldn't have loosened her hair. Instead, he thought the perfume was a waste of good money. It was expensive, worth a year's wages, so he said, "Why wasn't this perfume sold and the money given to the poor?" (John 12:5). It appeared to be a natural concern for Judas, who was the treasurer and perhaps often made suggestions about how to spend money. But his comment came from the darkness of his heart. Later the others found out that Judas had helped himself to the money in the treasury.

Jesus responded, "Leave her alone. . . . It was intended that she should save this perfume for the day of my burial" (John 12:7). The word *burial* must have exploded like a bomb at that happy banquet. Jesus had told everyone why he was making this final trip—to die. Everyone knew that the Jewish leaders, only two short miles away, wanted Jesus dead. Yes, the word *burial* stabbed the hearts of those attending this happy dinner. The trip to Jerusalem was for more than the annual celebration of the Passover. Jesus knew he would die in Jerusalem. He had not forgotten.

But think of Mary's act. How perceptive she was! She had listened to Jesus many times as he talked about his death as payment for the sins of the world. She believed it, and she searched for some way to express her gratitude for the Savior's suffering and death. Imagine how long she had to save for this gift; it cost an entire year's salary! Yet her gift was only a small token of thanks for her precious soul, which Jesus redeemed from sin and purchased with his own blood.

Simon, Lazarus, Martha, and Mary all showed their love for Jesus by what they did that night, but Mary did it best. Her gesture came from deep faith in what the death of Jesus would mean. Mary understood! So do I. Yes, because Jesus died and rose, I have forgiveness and eternal life. No expensive gift, even if it represents a lifetime's wages, is enough to say thanks. Mary challenges me every time I think of her gift. I need to find ways every day to thank Jesus for suffering and dying in my place. Because he did, I will live forever with him and enjoy the banquet of eternal life.

PRAYER: Dear Lord, when I think of what you have done for me, I cannot find adequate ways to show my love and express my thanks. Lord, take my life, my hands, my voice, my money, my intellect, and all I have. Let my humble service be a sweet perfume that fills my house and my life with the fragrance of my love for you. Amen.

7

Hosanna to the Son of David

The next day the great crowd that had come for the Feast heard that Jesus was on his way to Jerusalem. They took palm branches and went out to meet him, shouting, "Hosanna!" "Blessed is he who comes in the name of the Lord!" "Blessed is the King of Israel!" (John 12:12,13)

Bethany was just far enough away from Jerusalem to give Jesus and his disciples some quiet time. It was too far for devout Jews to travel on the Sabbath. The ancient rabbis had set the limit for travel on the day of rest. If Jews went farther than the rabbis had set, they would be accused of working on the Sabbath. But about an hour after the Sabbath ended at sunset, people began to arrive in Bethany from Jerusalem.

Those who had not stopped with Jesus on Friday but had gone on ahead to Jerusalem spread the news in Jerusalem that Jesus had come to Bethany. As soon as the Sabbath was over, groups of people came to Bethany in the growing darkness not only to see Jesus but also to see Lazarus. That night in Bethany must have buzzed with conversation and excitement. Back in Jerusalem, the chief priests made plans to kill both Jesus and Lazarus because so many turned to Jesus in faith since he had raised Lazarus from the dead.

When the sun rose the next morning, the little village of Bethany looked like a busy market where the merchants were giving food away. People were everywhere—talking, listening, and waiting for a glimpse of Jesus or Lazarus. Ordinarily this day would be a busy time for Jewish families celebrating the Passover; it was the day on which every family selected the Passover lamb for their celebration. These people had come to Bethany to look for Jesus instead.

Jesus had come to celebrate the Passover. In spite of the opposition of the chief priests, he led the crowd toward Jerusalem. I imagine a spirit of celebration infected the crowd. It must have been as if all the miracles of Jesus, all his sermons, all his parables, and, yes, all the Old Testament prophecies reached their highest point, like one steady triumphant swelling of enthusiasm and celebration. Soon the crowd transformed the cry of the two blind beggars outside Jericho into a song of praise to the Son of David.

Just before reaching Jerusalem, Jesus stopped and sent two disciples to the little village of Bethphage on the Mount of Olives for a donkey colt. When they returned, some spread their cloaks over the colt. The praise of the people burst into loud and continuous shouts of hosanna as Jesus mounted the colt and rode on toward Jerusalem. Again and again the people shouted, "Hosanna! Blessed is he who comes in the name of the Lord! Hosanna in the highest!" Some spread their cloaks on the road in front of the colt. Others climbed the palm trees and cut branches down to spread before the Lord. All this happened spontaneously while the crowd ahead of Jesus and behind him kept shouting, "Hosanna in the highest!"

Some Pharisees in the crowd wanted Jesus to restrain the excitement, but Jesus replied, "If they keep quiet, the stones will cry out" (Luke 19:40). Then from the hillside, Jesus saw Jerusalem, the long journey's destination. From the Mount of Olives you can look down on the entire city. It's still a beautiful sight for any pilgrim.

Jesus stopped. Like so many who stopped to gaze at Jerusalem from the Mount of Olives and to praise God for a safe journey, Jesus stopped too and wept. His tears were not from joy over finally reaching Jerusalem or over the hosannas shouted by the crowd. Instead, they were tears of sorrow over the unbelief in Jerusalem. Below, Jesus saw the temple surrounded first by city walls and then hedged in by the temple walls. As magnificent as the sight was, the temple was the center of the opposition to Jesus. There the chief priests had resolved to kill him. Jesus was walking into the stronghold of Satan, and he wept for them, "If you, even you, had only known on this day what would bring you peace—but now it is hidden from your eyes" (Luke 19:42). What love Jesus had not only for us but for his enemies!

The hosannas continued. When the people of Jerusalem discovered that the one who raised Lazarus was coming, they went out to meet him. Then the procession made the last descent and passed through the gate and into the streets of Jerusalem. What a day! What an event! No wonder every gospel writer records it. On the day when Jews were to select the lamb for the Passover celebration, Jesus, the Lamb of God, came to the temple. He was God's choice, his sacrificial lamb, brought to Jerusalem for slaughter.

John tells us that the disciples did not understand all this until after Jesus was glorified. We have the advantage of looking back at these events through the eyes of those same disciples after they had understood it all. Palm Sunday was a great event because God's plan was only a week from completion. God had talked about it for centuries—as far back as Adam and Eve. Finally it was happening, and I understand. I am moved to praise too!

PRAYER: Praise and thanks to you, Lord Jesus! You are my Lamb of God. At times my praise grows half-hearted and thoughtless in the tedium of my daily routine. Help me, Lord Jesus, to understand that you will perfect my praise in heaven when I join thousands and thousands of your people to sing, "Worthy is the Lamb, who was slain, to receive power and wealth and wisdom and strength and honor and glory and praise!" (Revelation 5:12). Each day restore a sense of wonder in my heart that my praise may be sincere and heartfelt. Amen.

8

Nothing but Leaves

The next day as they were leaving Bethany, Jesus was hungry. Seeing in the distance a fig tree in leaf, he went to find out if it had any fruit. When he reached it, he found nothing but leaves, because it was not the season for figs. Then he said to the tree, "May no one ever eat fruit from you again." And his disciples heard him say it. On reaching Jerusalem, Jesus entered the temple area and began driving out those who were buying and selling there. (Mark 11:12-15)

After leaving Jerusalem, Jesus and his disciples probably stopped to rest and talk briefly at the Mount of Olives before walking back to Bethany. Judas remembered this pattern when he brought the mob to arrest Jesus. He knew where to find Jesus and the others because they often stopped in the Garden of Gethsemane at the end of a long day. It was a place for quiet conversation and prayer.

Early on Monday morning, Jesus and the disciples walked back to Jerusalem. The large crowd that shouted hosannas the day before was gone that morning, as if it had evaporated like the dew in the early morning sun. The road from Bethany to Jerusalem passed a fig tree. Jesus approached the tree expecting to find some fruit to eat, but he found none. A fig tree usually grows its fruit before the leaves come out again in spring. The other fig trees were still barren, but this one had leaves, which normally indicated the fruit had already come. But there was no fruit on this tree at all—nothing but leaves. It was green but barren. Jesus sternly rebuked the tree, "May no one ever eat fruit from you again."

In many ways the barren fig tree was a symbol for Jerusalem and the religion of the Jewish leaders. On one hand Jerusalem was a holy city—the beautiful jewel of Palestine—on the other hand, it was the seat of the cruelest and bitterest unbelief. The chief priests and

Pharisees showed no fruits of faith in Jesus. They were barren. Even many of the loud hosannas were only the leaves of a barren tree. In just a few days, many in Jerusalem would echo with loud, insistent shouts for the death of Jesus, "Crucify him! Crucify him!"

On this Monday morning, Jesus entered Jerusalem and went to the temple. Already at that time the temple was more like a market than a house of worship. Surrounding the court of the Gentiles, merchants sold the necessary sacrifices to be offered on the altar—oil, wine, salt, doves. Others exchanged the foreign money of the pilgrims for the Hebrew half shekel for those needing the correct coin for the temple tax. The noise of their bartering and haggling filled the temple. If anyone wanted a quiet moment for prayer, he could not find it in the temple. How easily even worship in the temple could be turned into a barren practice, without heartfelt fruits of faith. Religious activity and ritual—the green leaves—hid the concern for profit and greed.

Jesus grew so angry that he drove out the merchants. He overturned the tables of the money changers and the benches of the dove merchants. Jesus chased them out of the temple as much with his words " 'My house will be a house of prayer'; but you have made it 'a den of robbers' " (Luke 19:46) as with his actions. As Jesus drove out the merchants and overturned the tables, the coins fell to the ground and rolled to a stop, the merchants angrily protested, and the animals squawked. But then a peaceful calm replaced the noise. The temple was once again a house of prayer and worship, and Jesus was at once both the restorer of worship and the focus of everyone's attention.

From that moment on, Jesus taught in the temple. All day Monday Jesus taught in the house of prayer he had cleansed. The disciples and others sat and listened to his teaching until the late afternoon. Then, just at sunset, Jesus left Jerusalem, paused with his disciples at the Mount of Olives, and went on to Bethany and the house of Mary and Martha.

For the moment at least, the leaders among the people could do nothing to stop Jesus because they feared him. But there was another reason they could not stop him. The teaching of Jesus amazed the entire crowd of people. The leaders looked for a way to kill Jesus, but they couldn't find a way because all the people were so interested in what he said. How much like that barren fig tree Jerusalem was! Instead of praying, the people were interested in making money. Instead of listening to Jesus, they were interested in silencing him. All leaves, all show, and nothing more. They omitted Jesus in their religious activity and ritual.

How could they omit Jesus? He had made such a dramatic impact on the city on Sunday. His miracles demonstrated both his compassion and his power. Self-righteously these churchgoers felt they had no sin and believed God would accept their good thoughts, intentions, and actions. They did not see the cross as the solution to their sin and the empty tomb as their victory over death. Their religion was flash and show, feeling and power. Ours is not. It is Jesus, Jesus, and only Jesus.

PRAYER: Lord Jesus, when you come to look for fruits of faith in my life, am I nothing but leaves—a show only for the world to see? You loved me and changed me so that I might bear fruits of faith—love, joy, peace, patience, kindness, goodness, faithfulness, gentleness, and self-control. All too often I wear a church face that hides the sin and evil within my heart. Help me trust you and your love for me, an unworthy sinner, that I might bear abundant fruit to your glory. Amen.

9

By Whose Authority?

They arrived again in Jerusalem, and while Jesus was walking in the temple courts, the chief priests, the teachers of the law and the elders came to him. "By what authority are you doing these things?" they asked. "And who gave you authority to do this?" Jesus replied, "I will ask you one question. Answer me, and I will tell you by what authority I am doing these things. John's baptism—was it from heaven, or from men? Tell me!" They discussed it among themselves and said, "If we say, 'From heaven,' he will ask, 'Then why didn't you believe him?' But if we say, 'From men'. . . ." (They feared the people, for everyone held that John really was a prophet.) So they answered Jesus, "We don't know." Jesus said, "Neither will I tell you by what authority I am doing these things." He then began to speak to them in parables. (Mark 11:27–12:1)

At daybreak on Tuesday, Jesus again walked with his disciples from Bethany to Jerusalem. Jesus would spend one more day teaching in the temple. On the way to the temple, they passed the barren fig tree again. The disciples noticed that the tree had quickly withered—perhaps the leaves were already dropping off and falling to the ground. The tree showed the judgment Jesus pronounced the day before.

Sadly, this day in the temple would be a day of judgment too. It started out as a contest between Jesus and the Jewish leaders, who were scheming to discredit Jesus with their questions while he boldly taught in the temple. It ended in Jesus' pronouncement of judgment. From his judgment there was no escape.

While Jesus was teaching in the temple, a group of Pharisees and Herodians came and stood among the crowd, listening quietly. At one of the pauses in the Lord's discourse, they asked Jesus if it was right to pay taxes to Caesar or not. The question appeared quite innocent, but they were trying to force Jesus to choose between God and the government. If Jesus had chosen God, they would have handed him over to the governor, who could crucify Jesus for treason. If Jesus had chosen Caesar, the crowd of worshipers would have rejected him as a Roman sympathizer, or perhaps the crowd might even have stoned him for blasphemy.

Jesus saw through their hypocrisy and asked, "Why are you trying to trap me?" (Mark 12:15). He knew this question had come from the Jewish leaders, who must have been watching at some safe distance. Jesus used a simple coin to make his point, "Give to Caesar what is Caesar's and to God what is God's" (Mark 12:17). They walked away, amazed at Jesus' ability to thwart their evil intentions.

Yet they were not finished. Later in the day, a group of Sadducees came to Jesus with a question. The Sadducees did not believe in the resurrection, yet they asked which husband a woman who had been married seven times would have in the resurrection. Jesus sharply rebuked them, "Are you not in error because you do not know the Scriptures or the power of God?" (Mark 12:24). Then he turned to the Scriptures and cited the story of Moses and the burning bush. There God told Moses that he was the God of Abraham, Isaac, and Jacob. Certainly these patriarchs were all dead at the time of Moses, but not to God. Jesus said, "He is not the God of the dead, but of the living. You are badly mistaken!" (Mark 12:27). The teaching of Jesus astonished the crowds, but it only enraged the Jewish leaders. The Sadducees dared ask no more questions.

When one of the Pharisees heard Jesus silence the Sadducees, he posed a question of his own: "Of all the commandments, which is the most important?" (Mark 12:28). Jesus gave a wonderful answer: " 'Love the Lord your God with all your heart and with all your soul and with all your mind and with all your strength.' The second is this: 'Love your neighbor as yourself' " (Mark 12:30,31). The Pharisee who asked the question complimented Jesus on his response and said those two commandments were more important than all the burnt offerings and sacrifices. Then Jesus reached out in love to him and said, "You are not far from the kingdom of God" (Mark 12:34).

While the Pharisees were still gathered together in the temple court, Jesus asked them a question, "What do you think about the Christ? Whose son is he?" They said, "The son of David" (Matthew 22:42). Then Jesus posed an important question for them by turning to the Scriptures again. He cited the first verse of Psalm 110, which says, "The LORD says to my Lord: 'Sit at my right hand until I make your enemies a footstool for your feet.'" If David called the Christ "Lord," Jesus asked, how can the Christ be his son? We know the answer: Jesus was true man and true God—the Son of David and the Son of God. They did not understand, and no one dared ask Jesus any more questions.

It was clear that Jesus was still cleansing the temple. The noise and confusion of unbelief gave way to Jesus and God's truth. Surely all the enemies of Jesus would be put under his feet. These enemies among the crowds in Jerusalem would also be destroyed. But for now they stood silently in the temple courts, unable to overcome Jesus with their arguments. They were as mute, dry, and lifeless as the fig tree Jesus and his disciples passed earlier in the morning and, like the tree, would be cut down and burned.

Jesus came from heaven! He had authority to tell the world what God wanted people to know. He still does, and he still speaks to us in the Bible. If we are confused about what to believe and whom to trust, let's take a few minutes and read what Jesus says. Unfortunately, so many in the world still don't listen to what Jesus has to say. They would rather believe a philosopher, a prominent athlete, a talk-show host, or even their inner feelings and opinions. They still think Jesus doesn't know the answers and so seek answers from everyone but him.

PRAYER: Dear Lord, I am surrounded by strange ideas about religion and life after death. You are the way, the truth, and the life, and no one comes to our heavenly Father except through you. Help me to treasure the Scriptures, which tell me of you. When I am confused by religious messages that seem plausible, turn my attention to you and your Word that I might believe and have eternal life. Amen.

10

A Great Gift

As he looked up, Jesus saw the rich putting their gifts into the temple treasury. He also saw a poor widow put in two very small copper coins. "I tell you the truth," he said, "this poor widow has put in more than all the others. All these people gave their gifts out of their wealth; but she out of her poverty put in all she had to live on." (Luke 21:1-4)

This incident during Holy Week always amazes me. Jesus spent most of the day in the court of the Gentiles, but he apparently moved to the women's court in the temple. He found a place where he could watch the worshipers come and offer their gifts. All kinds of people came to the treasury and deposited their gifts in one of the 13 boxes or chests located there. Jesus noticed this woman and singled her out of all the people who had come.

She was not wealthy. Many of the others who offered their gifts that day were. We might conclude that most of them were men. The woman's name is not mentioned, but we know she was poor and a widow. She was alone, so it appears she had no family to care for her. She was responsible for making her own way in life, and the way for a widow was difficult, especially in an age without pensions, welfare, and social security.

When I think of this incident, I am surprised by the choice of Jesus. He singled out this poor woman. Of course, Jesus knew this incident would be recorded in the Scriptures for all ages. That's amazing too. He chose this woman and included her brief story as a lesson for me as surely as he intended this lesson for his disciples in the temple that day. Considering the circumstances, one might well wonder why Jesus would spend his last few hours in the temple commending a poor woman for her gift. Didn't he have other things on his mind?

Yes, he had other things to notice that Tuesday. All day long, the Jewish leaders tried to trip Jesus with their questions. Jesus knew what they were up to. He knew his own time among these people was limited. He had a clear and unclouded vision of what would happen in the next few days. Many sat near him, listening to him as he taught. He was busy scolding the Jews for their unbelief and, at the same time, attempting to nourish the faith of his disciples and those who believed in him. Yet Jesus noticed this woman.

This lesson is an amazing little gem in the dark account of the Jewish plot to kill Jesus and their obstinate unbelief. The widow was a believer, while the Jewish leaders, who were generally rich and powerful, had rejected the Lord Jehovah. Quietly, alone, and without the notice of anyone else, she confessed her faith in the Lord. Her heart was filled with absolute trust and love.

She dropped into the treasury two small coins, an insignificant amount. Those coins represented less than a penny to the accountants of the day, but they represented much more to her and to Jesus. They were all she had to make ends meet. She did not hold back one of them for herself. She gave them both. They were all her earthly treasure, her "last penny."

To Jesus those two coins were a confession of trust in the Lord to provide for her. She put herself in the hands of God and trusted in his promises to care for her. Jesus had taught that lesson early in his ministry: "Look at the birds of the air; they do not sow or reap or store away in barns, and yet your heavenly Father feeds them. Are you not much more valuable than they?" (Matthew 6:26). She did not depend on her family, her neighbors, or her money-management skills. She gave God all she had and depended on him to care for her. So Jesus noticed and found this simple act a wonderful fruit of faith in the temple. It was certainly more than just leaves.

Her action was a testimony to the power of God. She believed by the power of God, and God the Holy Spirit kept her faith alive even in the midst of the tragedies and troubles of her life. In the midst of all the unbelief in the temple, a widow, no doubt missing her husband and, without him or anyone else, facing an uncertain and difficult future, trusted God. So often we find that the Lord works in the hearts of simple, humble people. They lack the power, wealth, and prestige of the world, but God continues to work in their hearts. It's been that way for centuries.

So often I need to relearn the lesson about trust that the poor widow teaches. When I worry about the future, God encourages me to put everything in his hands. When I try to figure out how all the bills will be paid, I simply must trust God to take care of me. That doesn't mean I am careless or foolish with the money God gives me, but that I have to put everything into his hands and trust. When I do that, I can give generously and joyfully. After all, this woman shows that giving is an expression of trust in God and his promises. It is also an expression of thanks for all the blessings he has given.

PRAYER: Dear Lord, so often I am tempted to give grudgingly and sparingly. My sinful flesh tempts me to think I have to keep my money for a rainy day or some new expense. So I give you what I have left over after I have taken care of myself first. Help me trust in you and your care, that I may put you first instead of last when I bring offerings to your house. Remind me of your great love for me. Then I can give an offering in keeping with my income that is a joyful and generous expression of thanks for all your blessings. Amen.

11

Last Words in the Temple

Even after Jesus had done all these miraculous signs in their presence, they still would not believe in him. This was to fulfill the word of Isaiah the prophet: "Lord, who has believed our message and to whom has the arm of the Lord been revealed?" (John 12:37,38)

All day Tuesday Jesus taught the people in the courts of the temple. He did not hide in the shadows made by the morning and afternoon sun. Although he taught openly, the Jewish leaders could not stop him. They stood on the edge of the crowds, watching and listening too, but they only grew firmer in their resolve to kill him.

Sometime during the day, Jesus began to teach the crowds with parables. He had taught parables before, but the parables on this day were stories of warning for the chief priests, scribes, and Pharisees. One of the parables told of a landowner who planted a vineyard, put a wall around it, dug a winepress, and built a watchtower. Then he rented the vineyard out to others. When harvesttime came, the landowner sent his servants to collect his portion of the crop. The tenants mistreated every servant the owner sent. Finally, when he sent his own son to them, the tenants killed the son (Matthew 21:33-44).

This parable summarized the long history of Israel and pointed to the plot to kill Jesus. In spite of all God did for his people, they killed the prophets and mistreated every servant he sent them. Interestingly, the parable was an adaptation of one found in Isaiah 5. There Isaiah wrote about a vineyard on a fertile hillside. The Lord cleared the land of stones, planted it with the choicest vines, built a watchtower, and cut out a winepress. But that vineyard produced only bad fruit—unbelief. Anyone who knew the prophet Isaiah, as all the scribes and Pharisees did, would know that Jesus adapted

Isaiah's prophecy. Clearly, Jesus accused the leaders listening to him that afternoon of being no better than the Jews centuries earlier who had turned away from the Lord. They did not produce the fruit of faith. They were all show.

Those who had asked many questions earlier in the day knew Jesus was talking about them. There was no mistake. The parable made it clear that Jesus also knew what they were up to—kill the son. Jesus ended the parable with the warning of a coming judgment on all who rejected him. He said, "Therefore I tell you that the kingdom of God will be taken away from you and given to a people who will produce its fruit" (Matthew 21:43). Neither the parable nor the warning changed the minds of these leaders; they renewed their effort to arrest Jesus but could not openly attack him because so many people thought he was a prophet.

Finally, in the late afternoon light, Jesus spoke his final words in the temple courts. Clearly and firmly he warned the teachers of the law and the Pharisees of their hypocrisy (Matthew 23:13-36). The sharp sting of his harsh words should have shocked them to reconsider their opposition and unbelief. "Woe to you, teachers of the law and Pharisees, you hypocrites!" (verse 13). He didn't say it just once but again and again. "Woe to you, teachers of the law and Pharisees, you hypocrites!" (verse 15). "Woe to you, blind guides!" (verse 16). "You snakes! You brood of vipers!" (verse 33). He spoke those strong words plainly and bluntly. And then he spoke of the coming judgment upon their unbelief: "How will you escape being condemned to hell?" (verse 33). I can imagine the teachers of the law and the Pharisees standing there with fists clinched and teeth gnashing. They must have stared angrily at Jesus as if they could spit fire at him.

As sharp as these last words were, Jesus concluded by expressing his deep love even for those who desired his death. He said, "O Jerusalem, Jerusalem, you who kill the prophets and stone those sent to you, how often I have longed to gather your children together, as a hen gathers her chicks under her wings, but you were not willing" (Matthew 23:37). Jesus longed to embrace and forgive his enemies, but they persisted in their hatred and envy. Earlier in the day he had disarmed their arguments. Then he warned them by parables, and finally, when everything else failed, he unmistakably announced terrible judgment. Nothing more could be done. His public ministry was at an end.

God always deals with people in this way. Gently at first he calls to them as the landowner sent his servants to the tenants. Some are always ready to listen to the gentle invitation of Jesus, but others resist. When those who do not listen persist in unbelief, the Lord repeats his gracious message. If there is no response, the words gradually grow harsher and harsher. If unbelief continues, finally the Lord can do nothing else but announce his dreadful judgment on unbelief. Yet even in that shocking announcement, the voice of Jesus reaches out to encourage repentance and offer forgiveness. He never rejects anyone who comes—only those who remain unbelievers in spite of all his loving and patient efforts.

That's what happened in the temple two days before the Passover. Late in the day, Jesus left. His last words were harsh words of judgment. And clearly there was no other way to deal with the unbelief of the Jewish leaders.

PRAYER: Dear Lord, I know how difficult it is to admit my own sins and failings. I have a tendency to defend my sinful actions and thoughts rather than confess them. Yet when you call to me in your Word and accuse me of sin, you desire me to repent, turn away from my sin, and trust in you for forgiveness. Do not let me defend my sin and produce the bad fruit of unbelief in my heart. Do not let me grow angry at those you send to speak to me of sin—my sin. When I confess my sin, may I hear the gentle and soothing message of forgiveness—my forgiveness. Amen.

12

Jerusalem in Darkness

Jesus left the temple and was walking away when his disciples came up to him to call his attention to its buildings. "Do you see all these things?" he asked. "I tell you the truth, not one stone here will be left on another; every one will be thrown down." As Jesus was sitting on the Mount of Olives, the disciples came to him privately. "Tell us," they said, "when will this happen, and what will be the sign of your coming and of the end of the age?" (Matthew 24:1-3)

For thousands of pilgrims, including the disciples, it was not difficult to be impressed with Jerusalem at Passover time. Besides the thrill of traveling to Jerusalem to celebrate the anniversary of Israel's deliverance from slavery in Egypt, Herod's building projects had made both the temple and the rest of the city a magnificent sight. It was perhaps especially impressive from the Mount of Olives, which still provides a spectacular view of the city.

Jesus and the disciples left the temple and began the walk to Bethany. Several of the disciples approached Jesus and marveled at the beauty of Jerusalem: "Look, Teacher! What massive stones! What magnificent buildings!" (Mark 13:1). But Jesus did not respond the way they expected. He said, "Do you see all these great buildings? . . . Not one stone here will be left on another; every one will be thrown down." Jesus saw things much differently. He looked beyond the stones and beheld the unbelief in the city. He looked ahead in history and saw the Roman legions marching against Jerusalem because the city rejected him. As impressive as those buildings might have been, Jesus knew that without faith it was impossible to please God. He looked beneath the outward facade and into the heart. He saw human history not as a record of accomplishments and failures but as an unfolding story of those who believed and those who did not.

I like to think that Jesus paused at the Mount of Olives as the light of day was just giving way to the darkness, at twilight. From the Mount of Olives, he and his disciples could see the entire city of Jerusalem silhouetted against the deepening darkness of the sky. They could see the temple; it was right in front of them, next to the eastern wall, like a city within a city. Its outer wall separated the temple from the rest of the city. The temple itself was made of white marble and covered with plates of gold. In the light of the sunset, the view must have been breathtaking.

The Roman fortress of Antonia stood ominously attached to the upper right of the temple outer wall. To the left of the temple, city houses surrounded Herod's hippodrome and theater, which slowly slipped into the shadows of another day's end. Somewhere in the city, Herod's palace rested quietly among the other buildings. Both Pilate and Herod had come to Jerusalem for the Passover. Because Passover was always a time of crowds and potential violence, Pilate had perhaps settled in the Roman fortress with the additional Roman soldiers needed for crowd control. Herod, perhaps to appease the Jews, had come out of courtesy and political necessity.

While Jesus talked with his disciples as they left Jerusalem, the sky became darker with each minute, and individual lamps glowed from the houses in Jerusalem and from the tents of the pilgrims outside the walls. The darker it became, the more light they could see from the wicks of thousands of lamps. Even in the darkness Jerusalem was impressive.

Jesus talked with the disciples for a long time. First, Jesus warned them to watch out so that no one would deceive them. He foretold the many false prophets who would come. Jesus knew they would deceive many people troubled by the wars, revolutions, famines, and earthquakes of the last times. Jesus said, "So you also must be ready, because the Son of Man will come at an hour when you do not expect him" (Matthew 24:44). Yes, Jesus will return suddenly, like lightning. Then he will judge all the nations of the earth. He will send those who did not believe "into the eternal fire prepared for the devil and his angels" (Matthew 25:41). On the other hand, however, everyone who believed will enter the kingdom "prepared for [them] since the creation of the world" (Matthew 25:34).

Jesus also told the disciples a parable about a man going on a journey who called his servants and entrusted his property to them. He gave his servants as much as their abilities could manage and then left, leaving them to use what he had given them. One of the servants did nothing with the talent he was given except hide it in a hole in the ground. Then the master returned. He praised the faithfulness of those servants who had managed his property well. But he condemned the servant who was lazy. The master ordered him thrown "outside, into the darkness, where there will be weeping and gnashing of teeth" (Matthew 25:30).

I've thought of those words when everything in my own world has turned as dark as that evening on the Mount of Olives. Yes, following Jesus is not always easy. War, turmoil, and conflict interrupt the moments of peace and calm. Pain, sorrow, and misery destroy much of our earthly happiness. The world still ridicules Jesus and persecutes his followers. In spite of it all, I cling to Jesus, trusting that he will return some day and take me home to live with him forever. All I want to do now is use the talents he has given me as faithfully as I know how.

PRAYER: Lord, in the growing darkness of this age, keep me faithful to you. As I await your return, give me strength to use the talents you have given me fully and completely. Make me a light in the darkness of sin, violence, prejudice, and hatred. I am your child by faith in your suffering and death. Use me and all I say and do so that through me your light may shine in the darkness and attract others to trust in you. Amen.

13

Money

Now the Feast of Unleavened Bread, called the Passover, was approaching, and the chief priests and the teachers of the law were looking for some way to get rid of Jesus, for they were afraid of the people. Then Satan entered Judas, called Iscariot, one of the Twelve. And Judas went to the chief priests and the officers of the temple guard and discussed with them how he might betray Jesus. They were delighted and agreed to give him money. He consented, and watched for an opportunity to hand Jesus over to them when no crowd was present. (Luke 22:1-6)

Jesus concluded his long lesson on the Mount of Olives concerning the last judgment by saying, "As you know, the Passover is two days away—and the Son of Man will be handed over to be crucified" (Matthew 26:2). Those words must have frozen the hearts of his disciples; they still did not understand. Then Jesus led his disciples away from the Mount of Olives to Bethany. As they walked, they must have passed the fig tree again. If it was still standing, it was unrecognizable except as a black mass.

In the darkness of Jerusalem, a group of men assembled in the palace of Caiaphas, the high priest. They met to plot the arrest of Jesus "in some sly way" (Matthew 26:4). They had long plotted his death. Their resolve, steeled with the raising of Lazarus, grew desperate. No light lived in their hearts. They had closed their hearts to Jesus, the light of the world. John, who later understood these events, wrote about Jesus: "In him was life, and that life was the light of men. The light shines in the darkness, but the darkness has not understood it" (John 1:4,5).

The heart of Judas was also filled with darkness, which began to grow slowly as he took money from the treasury. His greed grew until he was ready to betray Jesus. After spending three years with Jesus and witnessing his miracles, he turned on Jesus. Perhaps he thought this was an easy 30 pieces of silver. He may have reasoned that Jesus would never allow himself to be captured. Judas witnessed the power of Jesus many times. He had also witnessed the love and compassion of Jesus, but nothing Jesus said or did touched his heart.

The love of money is the root of all kinds of evil (1 Timothy 6:12). For Judas the love of 30 pieces of silver became the root of betrayal and even his own death. The tragedy of Judas is not beyond anyone. We may think we would never allow money to lead us to betray a friend. Yet if we pause a moment, we can think of examples of people who have allowed the love of money to destroy families, marriages, and all the people they loved. Sometimes people will sacrifice everything just to have more money.

Judas had been warned. Before his transfiguration Jesus told his disciples he would die at the hands of the elders, chief priests, and teachers of the law in Jerusalem. In his comments after that, he said: "What good will it be for a man if he gains the whole world, yet forfeits his soul? Or what can a man give in exchange for his soul?" (Matthew 16:26). Sobering thoughts, perhaps especially so when we think that Judas heard them. Yes, what good were the 30 silver coins to Judas? In less than two days, those coins would lie on the floor of the temple, and Judas would be remembered forever for his act of treachery.

I can think of many I have known who were more interested in the good things of life than in Jesus. They had time for vacations, fine homes, new cars, good food, and so many other things, but they had no time for Jesus. The temptations presented by life's good things are very powerful. I must never think the love of money cannot seep into my heart and life. Judas was a disciple. He walked with Jesus. He was there to witness Jesus' entire ministry, yet his love for money twisted his priorities. No one is immune from the allure of money. The cynic says everyone has a price.

How do we learn to follow Jesus and put him first? How do we trust that he will take care of us no matter what happens? Only by God's power. God reminds me that I am a sinner who deserves to be eternally cut off from him and all his blessings. Yet he loves me. Jesus was in Jerusalem for me. He carried my sins and received the punishment I deserved so that I could enter heaven and enjoy his blessings forever. He put me first. Because he loves me so, I can love him. I can put him first in all I do. Then whether he allows me to enjoy much or little of this life's good things, I treasure Jesus above all else.

The blessings Jesus gives me are greater than anything in this life, which is a short day—even a moment, a blink of the eye—when compared with eternity. Jesus has redeemed me to spend eternity with him. He gives me the spiritual strength and courage to love him. The best this life can offer is only tinsel in comparison to heaven. Because of Jesus in my heart, I put money, clothes, food, car, and house on my priority list after Jesus.

PRAYER: Again and again I hear the temptations of this world. From every side I hear the world, Satan, and my own sinful flesh telling me that values in life are measured by the amount of money I have, the car I drive, or the grand style of the home in which I live. Lord Jesus, help me treasure you as the only enduring blessing. Guard my heart from greed and the love of money. Keep the darkness at bay that your light may continue to shine in my heart and from my heart into my life. Amen.

14

Wednesday Quiet

When he had finished speaking, Jesus left and hid himself from them. (John 12:36)

When Jesus and his disciples left the temple Tuesday night, it was the end of his public ministry to the Jews. He was finished speaking to the chief priests, elders, and Pharisees in Jerusalem. His last words were words of judgment and woe. They had witnessed his miracles and listened to his message but remained hardened unbelievers. They wanted Jesus dead; they certainly did not want him as their Savior. Jesus would speak no gracious words to their hardened hearts again; he would not even threaten terrible judgment in order to call them to repentance. He left. He was silent. Mute.

That is a terrifying judgment. The word of Jesus is life and power. By the word of the Lord the heavens were made. By the words of God souls are converted from unbelief. When God speaks to us, he draws us to himself. Even when he rebukes us, he is like a loving parent who desires what is best for us. Just when God is silent, his saving work stops. He has bound himself to work through the Word, the gospel. When he withdraws the gospel, only sin and death remain. When he does not speak, men and women are left in their sins, and no hope of change remains.

The Jews, whether they admitted it or not, had become like Pharaoh. Moses warned Pharaoh again and again. Just when Pharaoh seemed to relent and allow Israel to go, he would harden his heart. During the dialogue with Moses, Pharaoh had continued to harden his heart. Finally Pharaoh stepped beyond hope and outside the patience and love of God. Pharaoh could not be touched by the words of Moses. Then God hardened Pharaoh's heart in order to bring about the deliverance of his people.

46

The Jewish leaders of Jesus' day had heard it all. Their hearts remained hard. Even one of the greatest miracles, the raising of Lazarus, only made them more determined to kill Jesus. Finally the words of Jesus could not touch them. They closed their ears to his message and refused to believe his miracles. Their stony hearts led to judgment. Jesus withdrew and hid himself from them. He spoke no more gospel to them.

On Tuesday night Jesus left Jerusalem. The Scriptures do not record his action or his words on Wednesday. He often went off by himself to pray. Perhaps that is what he did all day Wednesday. On the other hand, the Scriptures often place Jesus with his disciples in some quiet place. Perhaps he spent these last few hours with his disciples and friends in Bethany. They may have held long, serious conversations about the Scriptures, about the Passover, or about the events of the past few days.

In Jerusalem the Jewish leaders had time to convince the crowds that Jesus was a threat to their national identity. Caiaphas suggested that if Jesus was not eliminated, the entire Jewish nation was doomed. He and others believed that one man should die in order for the nation to survive (John 11:50). No doubt the Jewish leaders repeated that argument. Jesus did nothing to stop them. He stayed away. On Friday they would scream, "Crucify him! Crucify him!"

I think of the thousands of people who hunger for the message of forgiveness and eternal life. I also think of the thousands of people who have heard it so often they have grown immune to it. They don't find time to listen to Jesus. They believe they can do without the message of the cross. When people refuse to heed the gospel, it will be taken away. The Jewish leaders were not isolated cases. God continues to send his message of love and forgiveness to people. When that message is rejected, despised, and neglected, God withdraws it and sends it somewhere else. The great cathedrals of Europe are museums for the most part today. They are generally empty at the time of worship. How many believers in Christ can we find in the very birthplace of Christianity? Or in some of the early centers of Christianity—Antioch, Ephesus, Alexandria?

What a tragedy it would be for me if Jesus withdrew from my life! If I could no longer read his words of comfort or hear the gospel, my soul would die of starvation. God still works through his gospel. My faith cannot live without God's Word and sacraments. God works through them to nourish my faith and to give me strength to face life's unending challenges and troubles. When I sin, God rebukes me with his Word. It is painful to be scolded for sin, but God calls me to repentance because he loves me. If he stopped correcting me, I would continue in my sin and go unchallenged along the road of life to eternal punishment.

All in Jerusalem was not so dark, however. Before we take our next steps in this journey through the Lord's last days, we should remember there were believers in Jerusalem. Nicodemus and Joseph of Arimathea were among them. At the time they were secret disciples, "because of the Pharisees they would not confess their faith for fear they would be put out of the synagogue; for they loved praise from men more than praise from God" (John 12:42,43). We don't know what these closet disciples did while Jesus was in Bethany; we don't know what they did when the others argued in the Jewish council for the death of Jesus. We do know that at least Nicodemus and Joseph confessed their faith in Jesus at his death and provided an appropriate burial for the Lord of light.

PRAYER: Too often, Lord, I feel I can get by without your Word. Too often I am tempted to stay away from worship, and more often than I realize, I find excuses not to open my Bible. Do not withdraw your Word from my life. When I neglect your Word, call me back to your side and forgive me. Continue to speak to me in the Scriptures when I come to worship and when I spend time with you in my devotions. If you leave me, I am doomed. If you withdraw your Word from me, I cannot remain your child. I boldly ask that you keep your promise never to desert me or forsake me. Amen.

15

Passover Preparation

Then came the day of Unleavened Bread on which the Passover lamb had to be sacrificed. Jesus sent Peter and John, saying, "Go and make preparations for us to eat the Passover." "Where do you want us to prepare for it?" they asked. He replied, "As you enter the city, a man carrying a jar of water will meet you. Follow him to the house that he enters, and say to the owner of the house, 'The Teacher asks: Where is the guest room, where I may eat the Passover with my disciples?' He will show you a large upper room, all furnished. Make preparations there." They left and found things just as Jesus had told them. So they prepared the Passover. (Luke 22:7-13)

After a day of quiet, the disciples came and asked about preparations for the Passover meal. Jesus wanted to celebrate the Passover and was no stranger to Jerusalem at Passover time. The disciples had come here with him before, so sometime in the morning on Thursday, they asked what arrangements they should make for the festival. Since they were close enough to celebrate the Passover in Bethany and sensed danger from the Jewish leaders in Jerusalem, perhaps they thought Jesus might celebrate the Passover in Bethany with his friends. It was safer than going back into the city.

Jesus chose Peter and John to make preparations for the Passover—in Jerusalem. He gave them specific instructions about the place and how they would find it. Jesus demonstrated his ability to know all things and no doubt eased the fears of the disciples. Yes, the Lord they loved was in control of all these events. He told them about a man carrying a jar of water and explained to Peter and John exactly what to say. Of course, they found things just as Jesus said. Every detail was clear to Jesus.

Peter and John walked to Jerusalem to prepare for the Passover. They may have carried the lamb on their shoulders into the city. The law had clearly prescribed that the Passover lamb was to be a year-old male without blemish. According to the Old Testament laws (Exodus 12), they had chosen it on Sunday and killed it on Thursday. Jesus had come to fulfill all the Old Testament laws. He was perfect and without sin. He was the Lamb of God without spot or blemish—holy and innocent.

By our standards, the slaughter of the lamb was a messy business. Already at one o'clock the temple was filled with people bringing their lambs to be slaughtered. Peter and John stood among the large crowd waiting at the entrance to the court of the priests in the temple. When the trumpets sounded, the worshipers entered the temple courts with their lambs. The Levites slaughtered the lambs quickly, and the priests caught the blood in gold and silver vessels. They passed the containers full of blood down a row of priests until the containers reached the altar, where the priests emptied the blood at the base. Then the priests passed the containers back for the next lamb's blood. The lamb's tallow, kidneys, liver, and tail were burned as a sacrifice to the Lord. The priests and Levites were quite efficient in their bloody work.

When Peter and John left the temple with the lamb, they must have been splattered with blood. It was impossible to avoid being stained by the blood of the Passover lamb, and Jerusalem was filled with pilgrims whose clothes were spotted with blood.

In a wonderful way, I am splattered with the blood of the Lamb too. It is wonderful because I know the power of Christ's blood. The apostle John, who, with Peter, prepared this final Passover meal, wrote, "The blood of Jesus, his Son, purifies us from all sin" (1 John 1:7). My sins have been erased by the blood of Jesus. I stand before God forgiven, holy, righteous, spotless. I am washed clean by the blood of Jesus; by faith I have made the cleansing my own. That is wonderful and precious.

For Peter and John, being splattered with blood was not unexpected. For centuries God's people had celebrated the Passover. The festival commemorated the deliverance of God's ancient people from their bondage in Egypt. Every year the Passover reminded them of their deliverance, their salvation. Every year the death of the young unspotted lamb reminded them that deliverance came with a price. It required the death of a lamb and the shedding of the lamb's blood. All the other sacrifices outlined in the Old Testament law underscored the same principle: a person's relationship with God depends on sacrifice and blood.

John the Baptist clearly pointed to Jesus as the Lamb of God. He was God's choice. His sacrifice and his blood meant deliverance from a much greater bondage. Because of Jesus, the Lamb of God, I am delivered from the bondage of sin and death. Late in the day, Jesus arrived in Jerusalem with the others to eat this last Passover meal.

The lamb was bound in its own skin, and Peter and John carried it back to the house Jesus had chosen. There, over the hot glowing embers in an oven, they roasted the lamb without breaking any of its bones. They busily prepared the unleavened bread, bitter herbs, and a red sauce made from apples, figs, nuts, and cinnamon. They readied the supply of wine and arranged the furniture in the upper room for the arrival of the others. Finally they trimmed the lamps and set out the water for cleansing. Everything was ready when the temple trumpet blasts announced the hour of the feast.

PRAYER: Holy and merciful Lord, again today I find that I have sinned by what I have thought, said, and done. I have failed to do what was good and chosen instead to do what is wrong. I deserve to be punished for my sins. Yet I turn to you for mercy and forgiveness. You have sprinkled me with the blood of Jesus and cleansed me of all my sins. Renew my faith in the sacrifice the Lamb of God has made for me. Then help me, Lord, to respond in joy and gratitude as I renew my desire to serve you by my thoughts, words, and actions. Amen.

16

Love Serves

It was just before the Passover Feast. Jesus knew that the time had come for him to leave this world and go to the Father. Having loved his own who were in the world, he now showed them the full extent of his love. The evening meal was being served, and the devil had already prompted Judas Iscariot, son of Simon, to betray Jesus. Jesus knew that the Father had put all things under his power, and that he had come from God and was returning to God; so he got up from the meal, took off his outer clothing, and wrapped a towel around his waist. After that, he poured water into a basin and began to wash his disciples' feet, drying them with the towel that was wrapped around him. (John 13:1-5)

When Jesus and the others arrived in the upper room, they were safe from the Jewish leaders in Jerusalem. Not only did the instructions Jesus gave Peter and John demonstrate his ability to see all things, but they also hid the exact location of the supper from one who wanted desperately to know. Judas stayed in Bethany with the others. Of course, the room may have belonged to someone all the disciples knew. But even if the Jewish leaders knew where Jesus celebrated the Passover, they might not have risked arresting Jesus as he celebrated the Passover with his disciples. If word of that were to circulate, the Jewish leaders may have had a difficult time stirring up the crowd to cry for Jesus' crucifixion. Many pilgrims flooded the city and headed to Passover meals with family and friends. Whatever happened, the Savior brought his disciples to the upper room in Jerusalem for the Passover meal, which Peter and John had spent the day preparing.

When they arrived, no one offered the common courtesy of washing feet. Ordinarily a servant was posted at the door to wash the road dust from the feet of guests. But no one was there to wash the sandaled feet of these guests. Was it because the disciples could not decide who should do this humble service? We know they again were arguing over which of them was the greatest (Luke 22:24). Perhaps they were arguing on the road from Bethany, and the conversation spilled into the upper room. They might have been arguing over which disciple should have the position of honor closest to Jesus at the meal. Their pride filled the upper room with the foul smell of human sin.

This wasn't the first time such a dispute flared up in their conversations. While they were still in Capernaum, before the raising of Lazarus, they argued (Mark 9:33-37). In response, Jesus set a little child before them and reminded these proud men that if they welcomed a small child, they welcomed him. Then, on this last journey to Jerusalem, the mother of James and John asked that Jesus give her two sons positions of honor in his kingdom. The other ten were angry when they heard her request. Jesus again corrected them: "Whoever wants to become great among you must be your servant, and whoever wants to be first must be your slave" (Matthew 20:26,27).

The problem of pride persists. Like glowing embers under ashes, all it takes is a little wind to cause a burst of flame again. The words of Jesus did not erase pride from the hearts of his disciples. His words only gave them ammunition to shoot down the sinful flesh when it proudly walked through their hearts.

I know the problem of pride also persists in my own heart. Too often I look for the honor given by others and claim it for achievements I point to with pride. Our society is competitive, but that's not someone else's problem. It's mine. I want to be first, best, greatest. When I note the disciples in the upper room, I am reminded that pride existed among them too. We still argue over who is first and best. We fight for control and debate who gets the last word in our marriages and in our work. The church today is plagued by such contention as surely as the disciples were in the upper room.

In the upper room, Jesus taught humility with his words and then punctuated his lesson with action. He repeated the words he spoke on the road to Jerusalem. He told them, "The greatest among you should be like the youngest, and the one who rules like the one who serves. For who is greater, the one who is at the table or the one who serves?" (Luke 22:26,27). Then Jesus began to wash the feet of his disciples. He performed the lowly task a servant should have done.

Jesus gave another arrow to shoot down pride when it struts into our hearts and fouls our thoughts. The Lord of all the universe washed the feet of those he loved. His lesson is simple but often forgotten: greatness is measured by love and service, not by power and control. The church would run more smoothly if we remembered that principle. Marriages would cease to become power struggles. Work would be easier and more pleasant. Jesus loved us and showed us the full extent of his love by dying on the cross for us. That is his ultimate service to us. Our love, humility, and service flow from the love we have for him. Without love for Jesus, we cannot love and serve others. Without love, no position of importance and no accomplishment is great. If I could only remember that and put it into practice every day.

PRAYER: Jesus, the disciples argued over who was the greatest and best not once but several times. The sin that infected their hearts lives in my heart too. I covet glory and power, sometimes secretly. I become jealous when others advance before I do. Help me kill the sin of pride within my heart. Help me follow your example. Although you are Lord of the universe, you laid down your life for me and humbly washed the feet of your disciples as a servant. Fill my heart with love for you that I may love others and humbly serve them. Amen.

17

New Covenant in Blood

While they were eating, Jesus took bread, gave thanks and broke it, and gave it to his disciples, saying, "Take it; this is my body." Then he took the cup, gave thanks and offered it to them, and they all drank from it. "This is my blood of the covenant, which is poured out for many," he said to them. "I tell you the truth, I will not drink again of the fruit of the vine until that day when I drink it anew in the kingdom of God." When they had sung a hymn, they went out to the Mount of Olives. (Mark 14:22-26)

The blast of the temple trumpet signaled the beginning of the Passover at sunset. In less than 24 hours, Jesus would be dead, and those assembled in the upper room would witness his burial and then hide behind locked doors, fearing that the Jewish leaders wanted to kill them too. Only Jesus knew exactly how these events would all fall into place. Judas knew more than the others, but Jesus knew the plan of Judas too.

In that upper room, Jesus served as the head of the house. Assuming Jesus and the disciples celebrated the meal according to age-old custom, Jesus began the Passover meal that night by filling a goblet with wine and speaking a prayer of thanksgiving. Then Peter and John brought out the table with the lamb, three loaves of unleavened bread, bitter herbs, salt water, vinegar, and the red sauce. When the table was brought out, Jesus, again acting as the head of the house, read Psalm 102. The youngest in the company asked why this meal differed from other meals. Jesus then told the story of the Passover and concluded with the words, "So let us, then, say: Hallelujah! You servants, praise the Lord!" Then the disciples joined in singing Psalms 113 and 114. When they were finished, Jesus again offered a thanksgiving and passed a second cup of wine around to the disciples. Perhaps at this point Jesus interrupted the pattern to wash the feet of the disciples. He had waited, but no one washed the feet of the guests when they arrived and no one arose to do it later. It was time in the meal for the master to wash his hands—perhaps a good time to break and teach the disciples about humility.

When Jesus took his place again and washed his hands, he broke one of the loaves of bread into two unequal portions, dipped the smaller portion into the sauce, ate a piece with the bitter herbs and passed it to the others with the words "This is the bread of misery, which our fathers ate in the land of Egypt. All that are hungry, come and eat; all that are needy, come, keep the Passover." Then the Passover meal itself would begin. Some time later, it ended when Jesus broke off a small piece of the lamb. Then Jesus took the second part of the broken bread, dipped it in the sauce, and passed the loaf to the others, who did the same. Again the Lord washed his hands and passed around the third cup of wine, commonly called the cup of blessings. The group spoke or chanted Psalms 115 to 118 and shared a fourth cup of wine.

Sometime during the course of the meal, Jesus told the disciples that one of them would betray him. They wondered who it could be. Jesus quietly identified Judas, who left the upper room. His leaving would not have brought suspicion because the temple courts were open until midnight so that supplies for the feast could be purchased. Many poor came to the temple that night to beg for alms from the visitors who came to celebrate the Passover. The disciples thought Jesus had directed Judas to go to the temple and give alms to the poor. He did go to the temple, but to collect his 30 pieces of silver and a mob to arrest Jesus.

The Scriptures tell us that after supper Jesus instituted a new covenant in his blood—Holy Communion. Jesus took the wine and the unleavened bread from the Passover table. The new covenant in blood grows out of the old. The old sacrifice pointed to the events of the next 24 hours. The Lamb of God had come. The Passover would no longer point to his coming or his sacrifice.

The Lamb of God himself closes the door on the old covenant and opens the door to the new. We no longer celebrate Passover, but we do celebrate Holy Communion. This new covenant points us back to the Lamb of God, who took away the sins of the world. It is wonderfully new. The blood of the Lamb is in, with, and under the wine. The unleavened bread is the very body of the Lamb of God. We receive it together as the extended family of Jesus. He is still the head of the house, feeding us with his body and blood. When we receive this new meal, we remember the Lord's death, as Paul told the Corinthians (1 Corinthians 11:26).

Whenever I walk to the altar to receive Holy Communion, spiritually I walk to the upper room and join the disciples. Thousands and thousands of believers have made the same spiritual journey over the centuries. This new covenant ties me to Jesus, to his disciples in the upper room, to all the believers who have gone before me, to those who join me by receiving the Lord's body and blood, and to all the believers who will come after me. When the Lamb of God returns in glory, we will all be united in the grand marriage supper of the Lamb (Revelation 19:9) and sing the praises of him who loved us and shed his blood to cleanse us from all our sins.

PRAYER: O Lamb of God, I am unworthy to come to your Supper. I deserve death and punishment because of my sin, but you invite me to come. You offer me forgiveness and life in the bread and wine. As I receive your body and blood, renew my faith in your death for me and the world. I come forward with penitent steps that I may walk away forgiven and ready to live for you. Amen.

18

Anguish in the Garden

Jesus went out as usual to the Mount of Olives, and his disciples followed him. On reaching the place, he said to them, "Pray that you will not fall into temptation." He withdrew about a stone's throw beyond them, knelt down and prayed, "Father, if you are willing, take this cup from me; yet not my will, but yours be done." An angel from heaven appeared to him and strengthened him. And being in anguish, he prayed more earnestly, and his sweat was like drops of blood falling to the ground. (Luke 22:39-44)

The Passover meal had to end at midnight. The leftovers were burned, and a final hymn of praise was sung, Psalm 136. Both Mark and Matthew write that the disciples went to the Mount of Olives after this hymn. John records a series of conversations Jesus had with his disciples, concluding with a prayer (John 13–17). These conversations began in the upper room. Then John wrote that Jesus invited his disciples to leave the upper room (John 14:31). Jesus spoke the remaining discourses no doubt as the disciples were cleaning up and walking out of Jerusalem toward Gethsemane.

Jesus had come to the garden before. Each night when he left Jerusalem with his disciples to walk to Bethany, they stopped at the Mount of Olives for a time of quiet instruction or meditation. On this night Jesus came for prayer. It was after midnight when they arrived. If there were no clouds, the moon may have been bright in the night sky. It had been a long day, and everyone was tired. Jesus told the disciples to sit down while he went to pray. He asked Peter, James, and John to go a bit farther with him and watch. Then he walked away from them and prayed by himself. The quiet and the darkness were too much for the disciples. Their heads drooped down, and they fell fast asleep.

Jesus was in the midst of great anguish and prayed to his heavenly Father. Why this anguish? I always have answered that question by thinking of the burden of sin Jesus carried. I can never fully imagine what that was like for him. All I know is how heavily the burden of my own sins weighs me down at times. When I have hurt someone I love with my words or actions, I feel ashamed, guilty, and helpless to change what I have done. That burden is like a great weight that changes my outlook, erases my smile, and drags my spirit down.

Jesus carried that burden, but it was much worse. He carried the burden of the sins of the world. Multiply what I feel—and, I imagine, what you feel too—times every human who has ever lived. Imagine the terrible burden of Adam and Eve, who squandered the perfect world of God's creation with a sin of rebellion. That burden in some degree or another finds a place in the life of every human since then. That's the burden Jesus carried. I cannot fully comprehend it all, but I am not surprised that Jesus was deeply distressed and troubled.

Let me magnify that burden even more. Jesus was innocent. He did nothing wrong. He faced the punishment deserved by the sins of others. He was about to die for billions of crimes he did not commit. His anguish was so profound that he dripped with sweat—great drops of sweat like blood. We all sweat when we are nervous, but this was beyond anything any of us have ever experienced. Some suggest his sweat contained blood because of the stress of this burden. Medical history does record instances of bloody sweat caused by great mental anguish. But I do not wish to be distracted from my Savior's agony by any speculation. My heart, burdened with guilt, needs to know Jesus carried the weight of all sin. I can hear him moan in anguish, "Father, if you are willing, take this cup from me." He suffered as a substitute for humanity, as a man innocent of sin taking responsibility for all sin.

Three times Jesus spoke the same prayer. While he was in such agony, the disciples slept in the darkness of the garden. Even Peter, James, and John could not successfully fight sleep. When he came to them, they were sleeping. He left them and returned to pray. Each time he prayed, his agony deepened. The burden grew, but Jesus had asked for help and direction from his heavenly Father.

His heavenly Father answered. In the darkness an angel came to strengthen Jesus. He was not to die in the garden. Although the disciples slept, his heavenly Father did not. God's eternal plan would be completed. The will of God required the suffering and death of his Son, Jesus. There was no other way. So Jesus submitted to the will of his heavenly Father. He rose the last time, strengthened by the angel, ready to do as had been foretold.

When Jesus returned to the disciples the third time, Judas was already in the garden with his band of soldiers. Their lanterns and torches flickered in the darkness and woke the disciples from their sleep. The time was at hand. Jesus was ready.

PRAYER: Lord, I am very often weary and burdened. You know, and you invite me to bring my burdens to you in prayer. I know you understand. You have carried a heavier burden than I can imagine. When I am helpless to undo my sins or make amends for my failures, remind me that you were not helpless. You shouldered my burden and removed it forever. Assured of your forgiveness so I might rise and follow you again, I am ready to face whatever you have in store for me. Your will be done. Amen.

19

Arrested

While he was still speaking, Judas, one of the Twelve, arrived. With him was a large crowd armed with swords and clubs, sent from the chief priests and the elders of the people. Now the betrayer had arranged a signal with them: "The one I kiss is the man; arrest him." Going at once to Jesus, Judas said, "Greetings, Rabbi!" and kissed him. Jesus replied, "Friend, do what you came for." Then the men stepped forward, seized Jesus and arrested him. (Matthew 26:47-50)

Jesus stood ready to meet Judas and the mob. He was resolved to face what we all had coming. His robes soaked and stained with sweat, he stood before the mob Judas had brought. Judas had done his job well. It was long after midnight. No crowds would be there to see the arrest. Gethsemane was a quiet place, even secluded. Everything could be done as the Jewish leaders wished.

Interestingly, John tells us that the mob included a detachment of soldiers with their Roman commander. From the very beginning the Romans were involved in the passion of Jesus. So God had it planned. Jesus would not be killed according to the Jewish practice of capital punishment—stoning. He would be executed according to Roman law. No doubt, the Jews would have liked to kill Jesus in the dark isolation of the garden. Only a few months later they would stone Stephen in broad daylight without worrying about the Romans. But here the Romans prevented such an execution. Jesus was arrested and bound.

What irony! The Lord who made the universe was bound with either ropes or chains. How could these things hold him? His words made the dead live; Lazarus came to the entrance of his grave because Jesus called him. Jesus was not helpless here either. When they came, he asked, "Who is it you want?" (John 18:4). When they answered, "Jesus of Nazareth," Jesus said, "I am he," and the entire mob drew back and fell to the ground (verse 6). Jesus refused even the vain effort of Peter's slashing sword (Matthew 26:52-54). He told Peter to put his sword away and claimed authority to call ten legions of angels if he desired. The Romans would understand that. A legion normally numbered six thousand soldiers. Ten legions would be a force of 60,000. No match for the mob in the garden! Jesus did one more thing to prove he was not helpless. He reached out toward Malchus, touched the bloody wound Peter had inflicted, and reattached his ear, healing him in a moment.

These men were not taking away Jesus' freedom. He was giving it to them. He submitted because it was the plan of the Father. A few moments before, we saw him anguishing as a human in the garden, needing power from an angel. He is fully human. And here we see him healing wounds and exercising power over the entire mob by causing the men to fall backward. He is fully God. He set aside the full use of his power and majesty to sweat, bleed, and endure the rough hands of the soldiers. The Lord of all, yes, God himself, was arrested by a force of Jews and Gentiles.

The traitor had brought the mob to this place he knew so well. He had even given the men a sign. He would kiss the one who was Jesus so they would know whom to arrest. When Judas approached Jesus to kiss him, Jesus called him friend. Jesus still reached out to touch his heart of stone. The Lord was ready to embrace even this traitor with forgiveness. The entire incident became a burden too difficult for Judas to bear. Yet the truth was more profound. Jesus had already shouldered the burden of Judas' betrayal and would pay its penalty fully. If Judas had only trusted the Savior he betrayed, his end would have been different.

The detachment of soldiers arrested Jesus and marched him toward Jerusalem. It was the hour and the power of darkness. What were the disciples to do? Jesus did not resist. He told them not to intervene, so they vanished into the night. Jesus stood alone, deserted by the men he had chosen. One of them, Mark, only identified as "a young man," slipped out of his clothes in order to escape naked into the night (Mark 14:51). As the torches and lanterns moved toward Jerusalem, Peter and John followed at a safe distance. Jesus had told Peter he would deny him that night. Peter was determined not to let that happen. His sword proved his resolve to die rather than deny Jesus.

As I see Jesus led away with the soldiers, I marvel at the love of God for sinners. Jesus willingly submitted. He refused help from Peter. He did not call for help from his heavenly Father. He did not call down fire. He healed and then walked with them back to Jerusalem. He loved me enough to endure all this willingly. He loved these rough, determined men. He loved the traitor. I can only follow along and watch, marveling again and again at his love for all of us who have caused him this pain. His willing obedience is the only way all our sins could be erased.

PRAYER: You, Lord Jesus, willingly submitted to arrest in the darkness of Gethsemane. All too often I am asleep in the shadows, Lord. I fail to understand the depths of your suffering, the darkness of sin within me, and the riches of your love. Waken me that I might learn of your love and see the brightness of your forgiveness. Shine your love on my path that I might follow you all the way to heaven. If I am fearful along the way, Lord, do not let me scurry off into the darkness and be lost forever. Amen.

20

Before Annas First

Then the detachment of soldiers with its commander and the Jewish officials arrested Jesus. They bound him and brought him first to Annas, who was the father-in-law of Caiaphas, the high priest that year. . . . The high priest questioned Jesus about his disciples and his teaching. "I have spoken openly to the world," Jesus replied. "I always taught in synagogues or at the temple, where all the Jews come together. I said nothing in secret. Why question me? Ask those who heard me. Surely they know what I said." When Jesus said this, one of the officials nearby struck him in the face. "Is this the way you answer the high priest?" he demanded. "If I said something wrong," Jesus replied, "testify as to what is wrong. But if I spoke the truth, why did you strike me?" Then Annas sent him, still bound, to Caiaphas the high priest. (John 18:12,13,19-24)

More than 20 years before this night, Jesus had come to Jerusalem as a 12-year-old boy. When Mary and Joseph discovered Jesus was missing, they hurried back to Jerusalem to look for him. After three days they found him in the temple courts, sitting among the teachers, listening to them and asking questions. These men were all amazed at the understanding of Jesus. The high priest at that time was Annas. He had become high priest in A.D. 6 but had been deposed by the Romans in A.D. 15.

We have no way of knowing whether Annas was present in the temple when Jesus spoke with the teachers as a boy. But the Jews brought Jesus before Annas now. Why? It seems Annas was a very powerful man in Jerusalem. Five of his sons became high priest at one time or another, and Caiaphas, his son-in-law, was high priest when Jesus was arrested. Although the Romans had deposed Annas, many Jews may have felt the office of high priest was a lifetime office no matter what the hated Romans did or said. We might reasonably conclude Annas was the power behind the office even if he did not possess the official title.

Jesus stood before Annas. This was a preliminary hearing in the darkness of night. It was close to midnight when Jesus and the disciples left Jerusalem for the Mount of Olives. It may have been only an hour or two later when Judas guided the soldiers there to arrest Jesus. In the darkness Jesus faced Annas, still bound as a common criminal. No doubt, in another part of the high priest's palace, Caiaphas greeted those he had called to come for this hearing. While Annas interviewed Jesus, they planned their strategy.

Annas wanted to know about the disciples of Jesus. The disciples had fled, fearing these questions about them. Only John and Peter had found the courage to tag along to the high priest's house. From one point of view, these questions about the disciples were reasonable. What kind of men were they? Were they scholars? soldiers? rich? poor? Just who was supporting this carpenter from Nazareth? I would guess Annas already knew most of these answers. These Jewish leaders had discussed Jesus many times before, and they had even seen the disciples with Jesus. After all, Jesus had made no secret of his ministry.

If Annas knew the answers to the questions about those who followed Jesus, he likewise was not ignorant about the teaching of Jesus. Only two days earlier, Jesus taught all day in the temple. Both the Pharisees and their rivals, the Sadducees, sought to trap Jesus with their questions. So all these Jewish leaders had to know enough about his teaching to formulate their trick questions. But, of course, Jesus knew their intent and defused their pointed questions. For Annas, a man of such power and influence, it was simply hypocrisy to feign ignorance of Jesus' teaching. Annas was a Sadducee and perhaps had a hand in drafting their question about marriage and the resurrection.

Annas and the others still could feel the sting of Jesus' last words in the temple on Tuesday: "Woe to you, teachers of the law and Pharisees, you hypocrites . . . blind guides . . . snakes! You brood of vipers!" (Matthew 23:15,16,33). The sermon Jesus spoke on that day still rang in his answer to Annas: "Why question me? Ask those who

65

heard me. Surely they know what I said" (John 18:21). Annas didn't listen on Tuesday. He wasn't about to listen in the darkness of early Friday morning either. This hearing was just a stall, an interlude, without any value in any court of law. Jesus knew it. So did Annas. One of the high priest's servants became so incensed with the defiance of Jesus that he struck Jesus in the face. He lost control and violated an important principle of law: no one strikes a defendant when he makes his defense before a judge.

The slap in the face was the beginning. All would end with the death and burial of Jesus. Annas, as powerful and influential as he was, did not reprimand the man whose slap breached judicial protocol and etiquette. Jesus, still bound, was led out to the chambers of Caiaphas, who had prepared his case and his witnesses while Jesus stood before Annas.

PRAYER: Lord, I plead for mercy. How often I have slapped you in the face. My words of anger have screamed in your holy ears. I deserve punishment for them. My actions have shown a complete disrespect for you. I deserve to be bound. At times I have fled into the darkness of sin rather than be identified as your disciple. I deserve to be led away to punishment. Forgive me. I can say nothing to persuade you to forgive me, except to repeat your promise not to break a bruised reed. Forgive me for the sake of your love. Amen.

21

Known to the High Priest

Simon Peter and another disciple were following Jesus. Because this disciple was known to the high priest, he went with Jesus into the high priest's courtyard, but Peter had to wait outside at the door. The other disciple, who was known to the high priest, came back, spoke to the girl on duty there and brought Peter in. (John 18:15,16)

Peter and John panicked in the garden like the others and fled into the darkness. Perhaps they watched the soldiers bind Jesus and lead him off to Jerusalem. Both of them followed from a safe distance. It was not difficult to follow this crowd through the dark. They could see the light from the lanterns and torches far ahead as they kept to the shadows. The streets were quiet and empty, except for the noisy procession that escorted Jesus to the high priest's house. The destination was never in doubt; both Peter and John knew the Jewish leaders wanted Jesus dead.

The two disciples were following Jesus, but in a much different way than they intended. They did not boldly confess Jesus as they would after his resurrection. Then both of them would stand before the Jewish leaders and refuse to obey when commanded not to speak in the name of Jesus. Here they were creatures of the night, hiding in the shadows. They were afraid of being identified as disciples of Jesus. John was bold enough to follow Jesus into the high priest's courtyard, but not because he was a disciple of Jesus. He was known to the high priest.

I've always been curious about that relationship. Was John's family connected somehow with the high priest's? Was this a business relationship? Did John deliver fish to this house? Was Zebedee, John's father, wealthy and important enough to be included in some social, political, or religious gatherings? Was it something else? The pages of Christian literature hold some tantalizing opinions, but we just don't know. Whatever the relationship, it was enough for John to gain entrance and for him to talk with the girl at the gate so Peter could enter too.

The friendship of Peter and John is no mystery. They were business partners in Galilee. Both had brothers. Andrew, Simon Peter's brother, had gone into the wilderness to hear John the Baptist over three years earlier. When John the Baptist pointed to Jesus as the Lamb of God, Andrew brought his brother, Simon, to Jesus. Jesus called Simon *Cephas,* or Peter.

Two men heard John the Baptist identify Jesus; the other was most probably John. No doubt, he and Andrew had traveled together from Galilee to hear John the Baptist. Since then Peter and John were more than fishing partners. They were disciples of Jesus. For three years they listened to, watched, talked and walked with Jesus. They had grown closer because of Jesus, and Jesus had not only chosen both of them to be apostles but had also chosen them, together with John's brother, James, as his inner circle. How often don't we hear of Peter, James, and John! It is not surprising to find Peter and John in the high priest's palace, but we might be a bit surprised at how they got there. John was known to the high priest. His connection got Peter in the gate too.

When the girl saw Peter, she asked, "You are not one of his disciples, are you?" (John 18:17). Her comment implies she already knew John was a disciple. She must have thought, "Oh, no, not another one." Her voice betrayed her low opinion of Jesus and his disciples. She had picked up the attitude from those who came to the high priest's house regularly since the ministry of Jesus began. Peter felt threatened by her question and its tone and hid his friendship with Jesus and John. In effect he said, "No, I'm not one of those Galilean fanatics."

When I think of Peter and John in the courtyard of the high priest, I am reminded of the friends I have made because of Jesus. I am a disciple of Jesus and I have followed him, spoken of him, written about him, and listened to him. As a disciple of Jesus, I have met other disciples. I have grown close to some of them, and I would do anything I could for them. Like John, who was concerned about his friend Peter outside the gate, I am concerned about my brothers and sisters who are fellow disciples. Friendship in Christ is a rich treasure.

While I treasure my friends in Jesus, I also know that we, even together, may fail as disciples of Jesus. For all John's courage to walk into the camp of the enemy, he remained in the shadows that night. For all Peter's good intentions to defend Jesus, he denied him. I have failed to confess Jesus when my circle of friends includes those who are not disciples of Jesus. Like John, I am known beyond my fellow disciples. Every Christian has a wider circle of friends and acquaintances that extends to those who do not know Jesus or, perhaps in some cases, that even includes enemies of Jesus. Often it is easier to sit in the shadows and carry on polite conversations about the weather, family, or current events. I know; I've done it.

I too have followed Jesus from a distance like Peter and John. My desire and intention is to confess him before the world. But my best intentions often are not enough. I follow at a safe distance—out of the conflict and controversy. I find that I am not alone. Peter and John have walked this way before me. Yet Jesus loved them, strengthened them, and later used them to spread his Word. Later they stood before some of these same men and courageously confessed their faith.

PRAYER: Lord Jesus, I praise and thank you for my Christian friends. I treasure them as fellow disciples who also follow you and desire to serve you. Lord, you also know my circle of friends includes those who do not know you. Therefore, I ask for your strength and help. When I am tempted to follow you at a distance and hide my faith, strengthen me. First, give me the strength to live for you and let the light of my Christian life glorify you. Second, give me the courage to speak of the hope you have given me, whenever I have the opportunity. Amen.

22

Under Oath

*Those who had arrested Jesus took him to Caiaphas, the high
priest, where the teachers of the law and the elders had assembled. The chief priests and the whole Sanhedrin were looking for
false evidence against Jesus so that they could put him to death.
But they did not find any, though many false witnesses came
forward. Finally two came forward and declared, "This fellow
said, 'I am able to destroy the temple of God and rebuild it in
three days.'" Then the high priest stood up and said to Jesus,
"Are you not going to answer? What is this testimony that these
men are bringing against you?" But Jesus remained silent. The
high priest said to him, "I charge you under oath by the living
God: Tell us if you are the Christ, the Son of God." "Yes, it is as
you say," Jesus replied.* (Matthew 26:57,59-64)

The men who arrested Jesus led their bound prisoner from
Annas to Caiaphas. Most likely the route led only from one wing of
the high priest's palace to another. A courtyard separated the chambers of Annas and Caiaphas. As they marched Jesus from one place
to the other, they must have crossed the courtyard where the others
were warming themselves near a fire. Peter was among them. He had
come to see how all this would turn out. Those leading Jesus might
have jostled him and shoved him along; they may have already been
rough and impatient with him. The slap in front of Annas signaled
the beginning.

When Jesus came into the chambers of Caiaphas, he stood quietly and said nothing. Caiaphas and the others had prepared their
witnesses before Jesus arrived, and he paraded each witness out and
asked for his testimony. Something unexpected happened. The witnesses they had so carefully coached did not agree. Was someone
serving as a defense attorney for Jesus and cross-examining the witnesses? We don't know. But the gospel writers are careful to tell us

these witnesses did not agree. For Caiaphas the case against Jesus was collapsing. He could not make any charge against Jesus stick. Of course not, Jesus was innocent.

Finally two witnesses agreed that Jesus had threatened the temple. The implication of their testimony was that Jesus claimed to be greater than the Old Testament and all who worshiped in the temple. He claimed to be able to do more than Solomon or even King Herod, who had built the temple of Jesus' day. It seemed Jesus was attacking the old and was offering something new and different. But this testimony was not enough to convict Jesus either; Mark pointedly says they did not agree.

All this time Jesus stood silent. He did not offer a word in defense, nor did he scold them as he scolded Annas. The case against Jesus was slipping away from Caiaphas just as the night was slipping away. Caiaphas stood up and screamed at Jesus, "Are you not going to answer?" He could not take the silence of this prisoner any longer. Then he put Jesus under oath, "I charge you under oath by the living God: Tell us if you are the Christ, the Son of God."

The high priest wanted to know who Jesus claimed to be. Was he the Christ, that is, the Messiah, foretold in the Old Testament? Caiaphas also wanted to know whether Jesus considered himself the Son of God. Was he the Immanuel of Isaiah's prophecy, the child of the virgin, the branch that would come from the stump of Jesse? If Jesus said he was, then the court of Caiaphas would convict him for blasphemy. If Jesus said he was not, then everything he had claimed during the three years of his ministry would be a lie.

Men and women throughout the centuries have repeated the question of Caiaphas in one way or another. Jesus, who do you claim to be? Are you the Messiah or not? From the high priest's point of view, Jesus was an impostor, a threat, a charlatan who could do some amazing miracles. Caiaphas did not believe in Jesus and would not. But thousands in Judea at the time of Jesus and millions since have come to believe that Jesus is the Messiah, the Son of God.

Under oath Jesus told the truth, "Yes, it is as you say." For those who do not believe in Jesus today, this is just an example of perjury.

They ask, How could Jesus be the Messiah, God himself? But this was testimony given under oath. Caiaphas called on the living God as the witness to this answer as Jesus swore to tell the whole truth and nothing but the truth in any court of law. For me, the answer of Jesus is clear and unmistakable testimony. He claimed to be God. The question is always whether one believes his answer. I do.

Jesus stood silently before the accusations and false witnesses. He was innocent, holy, without sin. He was arrested out of fear that his teachings might overthrow the neat little religious organization controlled by the high priest, Pharisees, and elders of the Jews. He willingly stood and submitted himself to their judgment, although he had the power to destroy them all. He said as much: "In the future you will see the Son of Man sitting at the right hand of the Mighty One and coming on the clouds of heaven" (Matthew 26:64).

When put under oath, Jesus told the truth. The reaction of those who rejected him was great outrage. Caiaphas tore his clothes. Then like bullies, these men showed their power and dominance over Jesus, a power Jesus permitted because his time had come. They spit on him and abused him. By their standards, he was guilty of death. By mine, he is worthy of my love and service. He endured all this for me.

PRAYER: Yes, Lord, you are the Christ, the Son of God. Accept my praise and thanks for all you have done for me. Lord, keep me from unbelief. As I read the Scriptures, let me find you, the Messiah, in all its pages. Nourish my faith that I might love and serve you so that when you return on the clouds of heaven, I may rejoice forever with all those who love you. Amen.

23

No! I Don't Know Him

When they had kindled a fire in the middle of the courtyard and had sat down together, Peter sat down with them. A servant girl saw him seated there in the firelight. She looked closely at him and said, "This man was with him." But he denied it. "Woman, I don't know him," he said. A little later someone else saw him and said, "You also are one of them." "Man, I am not!" Peter replied. About an hour later another asserted, "Certainly this fellow was with him, for he is a Galilean." Peter replied, "Man, I don't know what you're talking about!" Just as he was speaking, the rooster crowd. The Lord turned and looked straight at Peter. Then Peter remembered the word the Lord had spoken to him: "Before the rooster crows today, you will disown me three times." And he went outside and wept bitterly. (Luke 22:55-62)

Peter was devoted to Jesus. He pledged to die rather than deny him. He had even drawn his sword and bloodied Malchus trying to defend Jesus. There was nothing wrong with his commitment to Jesus, his zeal, or his intentions. Peter was short on performance. After Jesus was arrested, Peter fled into the darkness with the rest of the disciples. But he stopped, and so did his friend John. Together they mustered enough courage to follow Jesus and the crowd at a safe distance.

When Peter and John arrived at the high priest's palace, John walked in unopposed because he was known there. Peter had to stand outside the gate. Before too long John spoke to the girl at the gate so Peter also could walk through the gate. It was late at night, and Peter could hide in the shadows. The palace was filled with darkness. For a time he stood inconspicuously in a corner or on the edge of a group. The courtyard must have been filled with small groups of men. The girl at the door was busy letting people enter. The high priest himself called these men to come in the darkness.

Those appearing at the gate were all familiar faces to her; she must have seen many of them dozens of times. She was like a receptionist who sees and recognizes frequent visitors.

A chill reached for those gathered in the courtyard, so someone built a fire to chase it away. Peter drew close to warm himself. But one of the servant girls saw something familiar about Peter. She looked at his face in the flickering light of the fire. Yes, she concluded, he must be a disciple of Jesus. A far deeper chill reached out for Peter—the chill of fear. He could not be identified as a disciple of Jesus here in this courtyard. His fear of being discovered erupted: "Woman, I don't know him."

The accusation of the servant girl didn't disappear as easily as Peter hoped. Another servant girl thought she also saw Peter's face among the disciples of Jesus. Peter thought he could hide in the darkness with the rough and tough men who arrested Jesus. His appearance must have made it easy to blend into the crowd of ruffians that night. But as he denied Jesus, he became part of the darkness. He pretended he did not know the Light of the world. Yes, he became like the others who circled the fire, warming themselves. He was safe from their accusations, at least for a time.

About an hour later, someone else challenged Peter. He pointed to Peter's dialect as proof. Peter was a Galilean. He did not talk like one born and raised in Jerusalem. They concluded he must be a disciple of Jesus. Peter must have talked in the courtyard, but we do not know what he talked about or with whom he talked. He talked enough that they could tell he was not from Jerusalem. Peter called down curses on himself and claimed he did not know Jesus.

Jesus had warned Peter that all this would happen before the rooster crowed twice. When the rooster crowed the second time, it was near dawn. Perhaps the sky already had begun to lighten in the east. Jesus was still bound. His interview with Caiaphas was over, and perhaps he stood in the courtyard waiting to be led to Pilate. Jesus turned and gazed at Peter, and that look chilled Peter's heart more than any predawn cold air. No fire could warm his heart. He had denied Jesus. Earlier in the evening Peter had boasted he would never deny his Lord and Savior. Jesus knew Peter had failed. Peter knew Jesus knew it. In spite of the warning, Peter had become part of the darkness. He had no light!

Peter was overcome with remorse, but all the remorse in the world could not erase what he had done. The gospel writers tell us Peter went out and wept bitterly. All his tears could not wash away one word. His denial is recorded in Scripture and will never disappear or be forgotten. Only the blood of Jesus could wash away this sin, this failure, this denial, together with the sins of every human who ever lived or would live.

How often I have found myself on the edge of a crowd of people, trying to hide that I am a disciple of Jesus! I have pretended to be like them when they have cursed and sworn by God's name. I have laughed at their crude jokes, not wanting them to know I was a disciple of Jesus because I was afraid what they might think of me. Jesus has looked at me too. He knows when I fail him. I also realize how helpless I am to erase one word, one sin. But I cling to Jesus for forgiveness so I might grow in faith and do better. I am a disciple of Jesus. I continue to follow Jesus because he is the light of the world, because he lovingly forgives all my failures, and because he strengthens me to improve every day.

PRAYER: Lord, do not let me slip into the darkness of unbelief. When I try to hide my faith and claim I do not know you, remind me of your unfailing love for me. Your look of love is worth more than a thousand words of approval from the world. Draw me to your Word that I may find courage to confess you before the world. Amen.

24

It's All Official

The men who were guarding Jesus began mocking and beating him. They blindfolded him and demanded, "Prophesy! Who hit you?" And they said many other insulting things to him. At daybreak the council of the elders of the people, both the chief priests and teachers of the law, met together, and Jesus was led before them. "If you are the Christ," they said, "tell us." Jesus answered, "If I tell you, you will not believe me, and if I asked you, you would not answer. But from now on, the Son of Man will be seated at the right hand of the mighty God." They all asked, "Are you then the Son of God?" He replied, "You are right in saying I am." Then they said, "Why do we need any more testimony? We have heard it from his own lips." (Luke 22:63-71)

When did Jesus look at Peter? Some suggest Jesus looked at Peter as the guards led him from Annas to Caiaphas. But others think Jesus looked at Peter sometime after his appearance before Caiaphas. In that case, Jesus would have been in the courtyard waiting to appear before the Sanhedrin when it convened again at dawn. We don't know for sure, but I like to think the eyes of Jesus found Peter in the early morning light sometime after the guards had abused Jesus.

After his first appearance before Caiaphas, Jesus was mocked, spit upon, and beaten. If Jesus looked at Peter after the beating, his face and clothes would have been wet with spit. His face may have already been swollen and bloody from the blows of the guards. At that moment while he stood in the courtyard, if Jesus turned to look at Peter, what a sharp arrow his disfigured face must have been for Peter. The look of Jesus penetrated deeply into Peter's heart. Jesus, bloodied and swollen, willingly suffered for Peter while Peter could not find enough courage to admit he even knew Jesus. What deep sobs erupted from Peter's soul!

When the cock's crow announced the coming of the morning, Jesus appeared once more before the Jewish tribunal. He had already been judged guilty by the high priest in the dark hours of morning. Then Jesus endured the mockery and brutality of the guards. Why the second appearance? According to Jewish law and tradition, a death sentence must be repeated on the following day. In addition, Roman regulations required that a sentence could not be passed before sunrise. So at daybreak, the assembled Jewish high court asked once more whether Jesus was the Christ. In his second court appearance, Jesus also testified to the truth—yes, he was the Christ, the Son of God.

He was still deserving of death according to this Jewish court, just as Caiaphas had said earlier. But remember the Roman soldiers in the Garden of Gethsemane. No doubt Pilate and the Romans had heard reports throughout the night about the arrest of this prophet, Jesus. The Jews had to be careful to comply with Roman law, especially since the Romans were already involved. The entire strategy of the Jewish leaders in arresting Jesus was based on preserving the Jewish nation. One man should die for the people, Caiaphas advised, rather than allow Rome to step in and destroy the entire nation. The Jews did not wish to risk offending the Romans and give Rome an excuse to destroy Jerusalem. If that happened, they would end up losing what they sought to preserve—Jewish identity. From God's point of view, all this happened as it had been planned. Jesus was to die a Roman death, not a Jewish death. Everything happened just as God had foretold it would in the prophets.

Early in the morning—very early, Mark writes—the Jews bound Jesus and prepared to bring him to Pilate. They needed to prepare their case for Pilate. After Jesus was officially condemned, the Jews might have met in closed session to discuss how to present their case to Pilate. While they prepared, Jesus stood bound in the courtyard, waiting to begin the walk to the palace of the Roman governor. In just a matter of minutes, the Jewish courts had finished with his case, and Jesus was handed over to another jurisdiction. Everything had been carried out according to the letter of the law. It was a great injustice, but it was all legal.

The Roman courts did not prescribe capital punishment for blasphemy. They did not recognize the crime of claiming to be Christ, the Son of God. Later history would record some emperors who claimed to be gods. The Jews could not convict Jesus of blasphemy in a Roman court. Luke records how the Jews changed the charges against Jesus so they could ask for the death penalty (Luke 23:2). When they brought Jesus to Pilate, the Jews accused Jesus of three capital crimes: (1) subverting the nation, (2) opposing payment of taxes to Caesar, and (3) claiming to be Christ, a king. For the benefit of the Romans, Jesus was accused of leading a rebellion against Rome and opposing Roman rule and authority. That was a capital offense in Roman law.

Jesus remained innocent. The Jewish leaders manipulated the law to gain the death penalty. Jesus was not guilty of the crimes charged against him. He was not guilty of any mistake, failure, or sin. He was the sinless Son of God, the Lamb of God without blemish or spot. Except to tell the truth, Jesus remained silent. He suffered the injustice quietly. He allowed the abuse without complaint. He did not threaten his accusers or the guards. He suffered willingly—for us.

———

PRAYER: Lord Jesus, how different you must have looked in the early morning light. Silently you endured the abuse of the guards. You did not deserve one blow, because you were innocent. Lord, I deserved each blow because I am guilty. Your suffering was for me. Help me, Lord, to find comfort in your suffering. I am completely forgiven because you endured what I deserved. Amen.

———

25

A King?

Then the Jews led Jesus from Caiaphas to the palace of the Roman governor. By now it was early morning, and to avoid ceremonial uncleanness the Jews did not enter the palace; they wanted to be able to eat the Passover. So Pilate came out to them and asked, "What charges are you bringing against this man?" "If he were not a criminal," they replied, "we would not have handed him over to you." Pilate said, "Take him yourselves and judge him by your own law." "But we have no right to execute anyone," the Jews objected. This happened so that the words Jesus had spoken indicating the kind of death he was going to die would be fulfilled. Pilate then went back inside the palace, summoned Jesus and asked him, "Are you the king of the Jews?" "Is that your own idea," Jesus asked, "or did others talk to you about me?" "Am I a Jew?" Pilate replied. "It was your people and your chief priests who handed you over to me. What is it you have done?" Jesus said, "My kingdom is not of this world. If it were, my servants would fight to prevent my arrest by the Jews. But now my kingdom is from another place." "You are a king, then!" said Pilate. Jesus answered, "You are right in saying I am a king. In fact, for this reason I was born, and for this I came into the world, to testify to the truth. Everyone on the side of truth listens to me." (John 18:28-37)

When Jesus arrived at the palace where Pilate was staying, he did not look like a king. He was bound and led like a prisoner. His face showed the marks of the beating he endured only a couple hours earlier. No servant rushed to offer him fresh water to clean his face. The spit from the guards already had dried by the time he stood before Pilate. His hair and beard were disheveled. Instead of royal robes, he wore an outer garment spotted with blood. His long shirt may have still been wet from the sweat and blood of prayer. If it had dried, it was stained. He looked like a prisoner—not a king.

The Jews brought this pathetic-looking king to Pilate. The first exchange between the Jews and Pilate revealed the tension between Jew and Roman. First, the Jews would not come into the palace; it was a place for Gentiles, and it was a place where these "ungodly Gentiles" would have yeast, or leaven. During the Feast of Unleavened Bread, such contact with Gentiles and leaven would defile Jews. It was Friday, the day after the Passover meal, but on this day Jews observed a feast of joy, the Chagigah. The term *Passover* often was used to include the Chagigah and the Feast of Unleavened Bread. The Jews stood outside, waiting for Pilate to come out. Pilate went out to them, diplomatically yielding to their religious traditions.

Since Pilate had come out to them, they expected him simply to order Jesus crucified. But it would not be that easy. Pilate wanted to know the charges; he was not going to execute a man without a trial. The exchange between Pilate and the Jews became a test of power. They wanted Pilate simply to rubber-stamp their decision and agree with their judgment. Pilate wanted to assert his power as Roman governor. Only a few years earlier, the Jews had lost the right to inflict the death penalty. At the time of this trial, executing a criminal was a Roman right, and Pilate seized the opportunity to assert Roman dominance in Jerusalem. The Jews acknowledged Roman power with the words "we have no right to execute anyone."

When Pilate looked at Jesus, he must have thought the charges were a joke. Jesus stood silently before his accusers. He was bound and beaten. If he claimed to be a king, Pilate must have thought, the Jews had beaten the idea out of his head. Perhaps Pilate thought Jesus was a lunatic, a harmless soul who had delusions about being a king. At the time Jesus certainly looked more like a lunatic than a threat to Roman power. The idea of being a king becomes one of the themes that runs through this portion of the passion history. "King" echoes through the accusation of the Jews, the abuse of the soldiers, the crown of thorns, the robe, and the words attached to the cross.

Pilate brought the prisoner inside, away from the noisy crowd, to question him. Jesus did not remain quiet but responded to the governor's questions. Jesus was a king, but not a king that would pose a threat to Roman power. If the charges against Jesus were true, his servants would have fought to prevent his arrest. But only the flash of Peter's sword in the garden defended Jesus, and Jesus told Peter to put away his sword. Pilate recognized the logic of Jesus' defense. He also realized that Jesus was no lunatic. The Jews had delivered him to Pilate so he would do their dirty work.

The road from Ephraim up to Jerusalem brought Jesus before Pilate. Jesus knew this from the beginning and told his disciples he would be handed over to the Gentiles. As ironic as it seemed, Jesus did stand before Pilate as a king, the Son of David. The prophets had foretold the coming of this king. The Jews read those prophecies and looked for political deliverance and independence. They longed for a king who would bring back the good old days of national glory, like the days of David and Solomon. But they did not read the prophecies carefully. The real King of the Jews did not come as a political, social, or national hero. He stood before Pilate.

Whenever I think that Jesus has come to fix all the problems of this world, I remember him before Pilate. And I remember his words, "My kingdom is not of this world." Jesus was not a political threat to Rome. He did not come to make heaven on earth. He came willingly to lay down his life. He came to take me from earth to heaven. He rules over all things so that I might join him in his kingdom forever. This is my king—my Jesus. I long to live with him but now serve him here, waiting for him to call me into his presence forever.

———

PRAYER: Lord Jesus, all too often I try to make you an earthly king. I see what is wrong with the world around me, and I long for you to come and correct the injustice, the violence, the bloodshed, the hatred, and the prejudice. Continue to remind me that your kingdom is not of this world. Lord, at other times, I place my hope and my happiness on the things in this world. I make you king of my world, expecting that you will preserve my health, my financial resources, and my earthly happiness. Forgive me for placing my hopes on the things of this world. Strengthen my faith that I may set my heart on the kingdom above, which you give to me and all believers. Keep me faithful and ready for your summons to come into that kingdom. Amen.

———

26

What Is Truth?

"You are a king, then!" said Pilate. Jesus answered, "You are right in saying I am a king. In fact, for this reason I was born, and for this I came into the world, to testify to the truth. Everyone on the side of truth listens to me." "What is truth?" Pilate asked. With this he went out again to the Jews and said, "I find no basis for a charge against him. But it is your custom for me to release to you one prisoner at the time of the Passover. Do you want me to release 'the king of the Jews'?" They shouted back, "No, not him! Give us Barabbas!" Now Barabbas had taken part in a rebellion. (John 18:37-40)

Pilate had heard it all. As Roman governor he sat as judge in many cases. No doubt, he heard all the defense strategies of criminals pleading their cases, just as judges do today. Some defendants professed they were innocent and claimed the Roman soldiers had captured the wrong man. Others pleaded for mercy and screamed pathetically as they were carried away by the soldiers to their execution. Still others stood hard and defiant when Pilate questioned them. In every case the defendant would put a bit of a twist to the facts in order to make it appear he was innocent or at least a helpless victim of circumstances. As judge Pilate had to sift through the half-truths and distortions to get at the truth. Court proceedings today are not that much different. The prosecution presents its case, and the defense presents a different interpretation of the facts. In our society a jury decides what is truth in criminal cases. In Jesus' day Pilate did.

Jesus did not twist the facts as so many others who came before Pilate had done. Instead, Jesus stood calm and resolute. If he did not look like a king, he spoke and acted like one. Yes, Jesus was a king. That was the truth. This King reached out to Pilate and invited him to become a citizen of his kingdom. Jesus said he had come into the world to testify to the truth and concluded his brief witness with the invitation "Everyone on the side of truth listens to me." The door stood open for Pilate to ask about the truth of Jesus. But he scoffed, "What is truth?" and went out to the screaming crowd to tell them Jesus was innocent. This opportunity to learn the truth of God's love disappeared.

The words of Jesus are truth. All who want to know the truth listen to him. His message is very clear and simple. About three years earlier, Jesus told Nicodemus, "God so loved the world that he gave his one and only Son, that whoever believes in him shall not perish but have eternal life" (John 3:16). That is God's truth, and it has been translated into thousands of languages throughout the history of the world. Throughout the centuries thousands have listened to the message of Jesus. Each Sunday morning the doors are open at churches throughout the world. Inside, the word of Jesus is read and sung. Christians have used speech, scrolls, printing presses, radio, television, and computers to share the truth with others.

But like Pilate, many thousands have turned away from their opportunity to hear the words of Jesus. Not everyone believes that his word is truth. Throughout the world thousands listen to the words of Mohammed or Buddha. They believe they have the truth. Millions find other things to do. They wonder how listening to the words of Jesus can help them find happiness and success. They listen instead to the gospel of hard work, which promises financial security. Sometimes they pay large sums of money to listen to business people tell their stories of success. Others listen to the gospel of pleasure: "Eat, drink, and be merry. Tomorrow you're dead." Still others are so busy they don't have time for the words of Jesus. All these people have adopted a different truth and ask: "What's truth? Who's to say your opinion is any better than mine?"

What draws me to the words of Jesus? Why are his words truth and not the others'? First, Jesus is God himself. He is King of all, Lord of the universe. He has absolute power and authority. He came into the world to share the truth with all the world. Because he is the eternal Lord of lords, I listen to him. He knows the truth. Second, his words always have proven to be true. He called Lazarus out of the grave with a word. He foretold the events of his passion before they occurred. He said he would rise from the dead, and he did. It all happened as he said. Third, Jesus is the only one who has offered himself as a sacrifice for the sins of the world. No other religious leader has ever done that. So I listen to him. He has the truth—the words of eternal life.

But his words have competition in my life too. Sometimes I get so busy I don't think I have time for Jesus. At other times I listen more carefully to the words of others than I do to the words of Jesus. Yet he stands before me and gently says, "Everyone on the side of truth listens to me." He holds open the door for me and invites me to listen so that I might live. When I listen to him, he strengthens my faith and draws me closer.

PRAYER: Lord Jesus, so many words enter my ears. I hear evil words of sin and perversion. I hear temptations to turn away from you. I imagine that I am too busy to take time to listen to you. But I am on the side of truth. You have redeemed me and made me your disciple. Help me overcome every temptation not to listen to you. Keep me close to you so that I may never turn away from you and miss an opportunity to hear the words of life you share with me and the world. Amen.

27

Innocent King

But they insisted, "He stirs up the people all over Judea by his teaching. He started in Galilee and has come all the way here." On hearing this, Pilate asked if the man was a Galilean. When he learned that Jesus was under Herod's jurisdiction, he sent him to Herod, who was also in Jerusalem at that time. When Herod saw Jesus, he was greatly pleased, because for a long time he had been wanting to see him. From what he had heard about him, he hoped to see him perform some miracle. He plied him with many questions, but Jesus gave him no answer. The chief priests and the teachers of the law were standing there, vehemently accusing him. Then Herod and his soldiers ridiculed and mocked him. Dressing him in an elegant robe, they sent him back to Pilate. That day Herod and Pilate became friends—before this they had been enemies. (Luke 23:5-12)

The Jews persisted. They insisted Jesus was deserving of death in spite of Pilate's findings. Pilate's interview of Jesus revealed that Jesus was innocent, but the crowd was not satisfied with Pilate's findings. It was still very early in the morning when the Jews accused Jesus of starting his so-called rebellion already in Galilee. Pilate heard opportunity in the accusation of the Jews. Galilee was under the jurisdiction of Herod. I don't know what Pilate thought, but sending Jesus to Herod bought him some time and had the potential of removing this troublesome case from the Roman court.

Herod was in Jerusalem at the time, no doubt trying to court the favor of the people so he might appear as king of his domain in Galilee. Many Galileans had made the pilgrimage to Jerusalem for the Passover. So Pilate sent Jesus to Herod, who was eager to see him. A squad of soldiers led Jesus through the streets of Jerusalem to the palace Herod's father built. Herod was not interested in the message of Jesus but only in his power to do the impossible. He had heard of Jesus' miracles and wanted to see him perform one.

Herod's father became king of the Jews when the Roman Senate set him on the throne of Judea. He had powerful friends in Rome and became their loyal friend and ally in that part of the empire for 33 years. He was ruthless in maintaining his title, "King of the Jews," killing anyone who threatened him, including the infants in Bethlehem. Joseph and Mary had escaped to Egypt with Jesus. When Herod died, they returned to Palestine but then moved to Galilee. Of course, that was all history when Jesus stood before the son of Herod the Great.

Jesus stood silent before this Herod. The Jews, on the other hand, screamed their accusations against Jesus. They reminded Herod that Jesus claimed to be king of the Jews and therefore was a threat to Herod's rule. Herod must have laughed at the ridiculous charge. Like Pilate, he saw no army ready to fight for Jesus. Herod's father had been proclaimed "King of the Jews" by the Roman Senate. Herod the Great fought battles to maintain his rule and built many grand buildings in Jerusalem, including the temple. This Jesus was bound, beaten, and alone. No one even fought to rescue him as they led him through the streets of Jerusalem that morning. Pilate wanted Herod to see this lowly carpenter. He was no king like Herod's father; he appeared weak and had no powerful and influential friends. Both men must have been amused by the irony of the charge of "King of the Jews" leveled against Jesus.

The irony was not lost on Herod. The entourage that accompanied Herod to Jerusalem jeered this poor "King of the Jews." Herod joined the mockery, and he threw an elegant robe around Jesus. It may have been a white robe. Great and illustrious men often wore white; it seemed to shine in the bright Palestinian sunlight. Perhaps this robe was one that Herod himself had used. After Herod threw the robe over Jesus, he marched him back to Pilate. The Roman governor knew at a glance what Herod thought of this "threat." The elegant robe was a touch of ironic amusement.

Pilate tried to talk sense to the Jewish leaders. He had examined Jesus in their presence and found no basis for their charges. Herod had also examined Jesus and found no reason for the death penalty. He was innocent! We know he was more than that; he was holy! Both men smiled at the charge the Jews brought against Jesus. In their world of power and wealth, Jesus was no king. Even the elegant robe did not make him appear any more a king. No army—not even a defeated one. No entourage. No treasury. No court. No glory. No majesty! A king? No wonder the soldiers jeered and mocked him.

But he was and is a king. Jesus told Caiaphas under oath, "In the future you will see the Son of Man sitting at the right hand of the Mighty One and coming on the clouds of heaven" (Matthew 26:64). We shall see him then, and so will Herod, Pilate, the Jews, and all who mocked him. Then Herod's elegant robe will look like a rag. Jesus will be "dressed in a robe reaching down to his feet and with a golden sash around his chest. His head and hair [will be] white like wool, as white as snow, and his eyes [will be] like blazing fire. . . . His face [will be] like the sun shining in all its brilliance" (Revelation 1:13,14,16). Before Herod and Pilate, he set aside that glory and majesty in order to suffer for me and all people. What love! What devotion to others! He is my King, and I bow before him in humble reverence.

PRAYER: Jesus, Lord of lords and King of kings, you set aside your glory to become like me. Because of your suffering, I have a place in your royal family as your adopted child. I am your loyal subject. Help me praise you always for your love for me and all humanity—a love that led you to humble yourself and endure mockery and jeering as "King of the Jews." I know you as King of all, and I ask that you would protect me and those I love from all that would hurt us. Preserve us in faith until the end, that we might receive the crown of life and stand in your glorious presence to sing your praises forever. Amen.

28

Here Is the Man!

Then Pilate took Jesus and had him flogged. The soldiers twisted together a crown of thorns and put it on his head. They clothed him in a purple robe and went up to him again and again, saying, "Hail, king of the Jews!" And they struck him in the face. Once more Pilate came out and said to the Jews, "Look, I am bringing him out to you to let you know that I find no basis for a charge against him." When Jesus came out wearing the crown of thorns and the purple robe, Pilate said to them, "Here is the man!" (John 19:1-5)

Pilate had no question about whether Jesus was innocent or deserved death. He announced his findings to the Jews on more than one occasion. He sent him to Herod, who also thought Jesus was innocent. When Jesus returned from the interview with Herod, Pilate again told the Jews that Jesus was not guilty. I think of Pilate as a man who wanted to free Jesus. Luke tells us Pilate tried three times to convince the Jews that Jesus was innocent (Luke 23:22).

When the Jewish leaders would not listen and insisted on the death of Jesus, Pilate took two more steps to satisfy the Jews and allow Jesus to go free. First, Pilate offered the Jews a choice: Jesus or Barabbas. This Barabbas was bad. He was a violent, brutal man guilty of murder and rebellion. Pilate pitted this man against Jesus. The choice should have been obvious. But the Jews did not care for public safety or protection from random violence. They wanted Jesus dead, so they chose Barabbas. Pilate failed with this way to release Jesus.

Pilate's second step was to have Jesus flogged. Jesus was innocent, of course, and did not deserve such a brutal whipping. Pilate may have thought the Jews would be satisfied with the beating of their "king." So Pilate turned Jesus over to his soldiers. They stripped off Herod's elegant robe and his own clothes so that his back was bare. Then the soldiers stretched Jesus over a pillar with his back exposed to the lashes of the whip. The small pieces of bone fastened to the end of the lashes ripped the skin and flesh of his back. In some floggings, the bones were exposed because the lashes tore away the flesh. When Jesus stood up after the flogging, his back was like a bloody piece of raw meat.

The soldiers were not done yet. They did not miss an opportunity to make fun of Jesus, "King of the Jews." Like Herod, they thought the charge against Jesus was ridiculous. He was no king by any definition they knew. In place of the elegant robe of Herod, they put a purple robe on Jesus. Purple was the color of kings. But this robe was not a royal robe like the robe of Herod. Instead, it was an old soldier's mantle. Its once-red color had faded and darkened with age. This mantle was as close as Jesus came to royal purple on earth. The soldiers also remembered that every king must have a crown. So they made Jesus a crown of thorns and put it on his head. The thorns were long, sharp spikes, not short, prickly tines. For a scepter they gave him a stick or staff. "Hail, King of the Jews!" they laughed and called out. Then again and again they took the stick and hit Jesus on the head, driving the thorns into his scalp.

When the soldiers finished making fun of Jesus, Pilate brought him out for the Jews to see. What a sight! His face swollen and distorted from the beating by the soldiers, streams of blood running down his face from the places where the thorns opened wounds in his head, his back bloody and raw—the scene was brutal and gory. Pilate hoped the sight would satisfy the Jews or awaken some compassion for Jesus. But it did not. "Here is the man!" he said.

I see Jesus as a gory, bloody mess standing before the screaming crowd. Yes, here is the man. But I find comfort in his bloody face. He came to suffer for the sins of the world. He came to suffer for my sins. Sin is not some small mistake that can be whisked away easily and forgotten. Sin violates God's nature; he is holy. It is God's nature to oppose sin and destroy it, just as it is the nature of our white blood cells to attack and kill every germ that invades our bodies. All my sins violate his perfect holiness. He must attack them and destroy them. Because of my sins, God should treat me as Jesus was treated. I should be beaten bloody for my sins. But Jesus has endured what I deserve. I escape God's wrath because Jesus suffered for me. I can go free because Jesus endured this brutal death. Jesus took my punishment; he is my substitute.

Pilate only inspired the crowd to shout louder, "Crucify! Crucify!" Pilate failed and finally made it impossible to release Jesus. Once he flogged Jesus, there was no turning back. As Jesus stood in the early morning sunlight, bloody and beaten, everything was happening just as he had told his disciples. He would be betrayed, turned over to the Gentiles, mocked, spit on, flogged, and then killed (Mark 10:33,34). I think of him before the crowd and exclaim, "Oh, Savior, Precious Savior!"

PRAYER: Look, the Lamb of God! Lord Jesus, I should be beaten because of my sins. I should be whipped. All too often I think my sins are little mistakes that somehow can be forgotten. I do not want to admit my sins; instead, I wish to deny them, minimize them, and excuse them. But each one violates your holy law. My angry thoughts are just as bad as the violent act of murder. In your wounds, Lord, may I find full forgiveness for each evil thought, each angry word, and each unloving deed. Amen.

29

Where Do You Come From?

As soon as the chief priests and their officials saw him, they shouted, "Crucify! Crucify!" But Pilate answered, "You take him and crucify him. As for me, I find no basis for a charge against him." The Jews insisted, "We have a law, and according to that law he must die, because he claimed to be the Son of God." When Pilate heard this, he was even more afraid, and he went back inside the palace. "Where do you come from?" he asked Jesus, but Jesus gave him no answer. "Do you refuse to speak to me?" Pilate said. "Don't you realize I have power either to free you or to crucify you?" Jesus answered, "You would have no power over me if it were not given to you from above. Therefore the one who handed me over to you is guilty of a greater sin." From then on, Pilate tried to set Jesus free, but the Jews kept shouting, "If you let this man go, you are no friend of Caesar. Anyone who claims to be a king opposes Caesar." (John 19:6-12)

Were the disciples somewhere in the crowd early in the morning? Were the two former blind men Jesus healed in Jericho still following him? They had all walked with Jesus up to Jerusalem. Jesus knew what would happen; he had told them many times. They listened to his words and understood the danger. Thomas had told the other disciples, "Let us also go, that we may die with him" (John 11:16). The disciples loved Jesus deeply and desired to follow him. The two former blind men came to Jerusalem and saw this take place. The others who followed Jesus watched it happen too. But they were all paralyzed by fear, numbed by the brutality, and unprepared for how quickly it happened. Only after it was over did they really understand why it happened.

I follow Jesus too. In spirit I walk with him each time I read or hear the story of his suffering and death. Jesus is my friend, and I love him because he loves me. Instead of shouting for his death, I imagine standing at the edge of the crowd, tucked away in a doorway or archway in the dark shade of the early morning. My eyes fill with tears as I hear them shout in anger to hurt the one I love. But I would stand unable to change anything. I too would be paralyzed by fear for my own life and stunned both by the brutality of the Romans and the hatred of the Jewish leaders.

But I also know that Jesus was not helpless. He caused the wind to be still on the Sea of Galilee and could have stopped the shouts of the Jews. He could have disappeared before Pilate's eyes or shackled the soldiers and frozen them in place. He could have done it all with a word, just as he created the world with a word. But he did not. These events occurred as he wanted them to occur. I would not want to change this history either.

When the Jews told Pilate that Jesus claimed to be the Son of God, the Roman governor became afraid. He wondered just who Jesus was. Pilate grew up in a world of mythology, where the gods often entered human history. If Pilate didn't actually believe the myths, he at least knew them. Perhaps Pilate thought for a moment that Jesus came from the gods. If that were true, Jesus could become angry and bring great suffering to him and his family. He renewed his interview of Jesus: "Where do you come from?" Jesus remained silent at first. Pilate threatened him: "Don't you realize I have power either to free you or to crucify you?" Jesus responded this time. He rebuked Pilate for his arrogant threat. Jesus did not answer as someone helpless and in fear of death. He spoke with calm dignity, as one in complete control.

Pilate returned to the Jews and again sought to release Jesus. The square where Pilate met with them was still filled with morning shadows. The sun had not risen very high in the sky, and the walls and buildings of Jerusalem cast long shadows in the cool morning light. I can imagine myself standing in a shadowy corner, trying not to attract attention to myself—hiding in plain sight. Pilate argued with the Jews while Jesus stood there, quiet, bloody, and crowned with thorns.

Where does Jesus come from? He comes from above. He is not just a man. He is God—not the like the gods of the Romans and Greeks, but the Lord God of the Jews. Isaiah wrote centuries before Jesus came, "He was pierced for our transgressions, he was crushed for our iniquities; the punishment that brought us peace was upon him, and by his wounds we are healed" (Isaiah 53:5). Jesus suffered for all the world. One man's sacrifice is not enough for that. Jesus' sacrifice must be worth more. He is God, and therefore his death is enough to pay for all the world's violence, bloodshed, crime, and immorality.

Throughout the centuries men and women have argued over whether Jesus is divine and in what sense he is God. This has not been an argument over trivialities or of splitting theological hairs. If Jesus is God himself, the one true God of the Bible, his suffering pays for the sins of all humanity. If he was only a man—even an innocent, decent man who endured injustice—his suffering cannot cleanse. It only provides an example of endurance and dignity under pressure. But Jesus is God! He is God from God, Light from Light, true God from true God. His one death was enough to pay for all sins.

PRAYER: Dearest Jesus, you have opened my eyes to see that you are the Lord of heaven, the Son of God, come to earth for me and for all humanity. Let me find comfort in your precious blood. It is sacrifice enough to remove my darkest sin. Your precious blood cleanses me that I might stand before you forever—forgiven and pure. Take me from the shadows and help me boldly proclaim your love to others. Amen.

30

Sentenced to Death

*When Pilate saw that he was getting nowhere, but that instead
an uproar was starting, he took water and washed his hands in
front of the crowd. "I am innocent of this man's blood," he said.
"It is your responsibility!" All the people answered, "Let his
blood be on us and on our children!"* (Matthew 27:24,25)

No way out! For Pilate it became painfully clear. Jesus was innocent. He did not deserve death. Every time he tried to release Jesus,
Pilate was frustrated. Not only did he know that Jesus was innocent,
but his wife sent word that she had suffered in a dream because of
Jesus. Her message was simple, "Don't have anything to do with that
innocent man, for I have suffered a great deal today in a dream
because of him" (Matthew 27:19). Her message must have confirmed
Pilate's fear that Jesus was more than just a man. But Pilate could
find no way out.

Pilate was a practical Roman. The emperor sent him to Judea to
assert Roman power and justice. He was, like most Romans, moti-
vated by duty and honor. Jesus was innocent; it was Pilate's duty to
release him. But Pilate was also a realist. After all his efforts to
release Jesus, it appeared that the controversy over Jesus threatened
to turn into a riot. To Pilate, Jerusalem appeared for a moment to
teeter on the brink of civil unrest. If a riot occurred, no doubt Pilate
thought it would turn ugly and bloody. If that happened, he would
send Roman soldiers into the streets, and the soldiers would do
whatever was necessary to restore order. That meant the possibility
of bloodshed on both sides. He must avoid that if at all possible.

To make matters worse, the Jews threatened: "If you let this man
go, you are no friend of Caesar. Anyone who claims to be a king
opposes Caesar" (John 19:12). These words made Pilate's decision
easy. If Caesar would review the release of Jesus, the Jews would

charge Pilate with dereliction of duty. After all, they would claim Pilate released a man who claimed to be a king, a traitor to Rome. Pilate's career would take a dive. He would no longer be a friend of Caesar. On the other hand, if Pilate gave the order to crucify Jesus, he could easily claim he had executed an enemy of Rome, and the Jews would support his claim. When Pilate still protested, the Jews claimed, "We have no king but Caesar" (John 19:15).

Pilate's sense of honor and duty were not easily overcome. He did not want to be a party to the death of an innocent carpenter from Galilee. Although he issued the order to crucify Jesus, he publicly washed his hands and proclaimed his own innocence. He had made a political decision. He did not risk a riot and bloodshed in the streets of Jerusalem in order to release Jesus. Neither did he risk his own future. He was not willing to appear to be befriending an enemy of Rome whom the Jews themselves accused with treason and rebellion as the "King of the Jews." For a little over two hours, Pilate fought with the Jews for the release of Jesus, but in the end he issued the order for crucifixion. His name will forever be tied to this injustice, as Christians confess that Jesus "suffered under Pontius Pilate."

Pilate chose his career instead of Jesus. When the Lord Jesus stood before him, Pilate chose to appease the Jews and crucify the Savior of the world. He had no spiritual vision. From his perspective his decision made sense. He did not recognize Jesus as King and Lord. Peace, quiet, tranquillity, and a secure future in the Roman Empire were more important in his world than what Jesus could give him: forgiveness, life, and paradise. Even though Pilate may have wondered whether Jesus' claims were true, order and peace in Jerusalem at the Passover were more important. Because he did not see Jesus as his Savior, Pilate set aside his sense of duty and honor. If he had seen Jesus as Lord God Almighty, he wouldn't have issued the order for Jesus' crucifixion.

The world is still full of Pilates, who do not see Jesus. So many have no spiritual vision. They do not see Jesus as Lord, Savior, King, Friend, and Master. He is not important in their lives. Instead, careers become more important than Jesus. If one has no spiritual vision, then one has no time for Jesus and the Bible. Money becomes God instead of Jesus. Work and financial security occupy so much time and energy that there is none left even for one hour a week with Jesus. If they knew that Jesus is the loving Lord Almighty, they would change their priorities.

I am a disciple of Jesus, and yet I know my spiritual vision becomes cloudy. Jesus, at times, seems so far away. I don't see him as clearly as I should. When that happens, I treasure the things of this world more than Jesus. I do what pleases others rather than what pleases him. I must look more carefully at Jesus. He stood beaten and bloody next to Pilate so that I would have forgiveness, life, and paradise. Each day I repent of my cloudy spiritual vision and wipe it clear with the suffering and death of Jesus.

PRAYER: Lord, forgive me when my vision is clouded by the cares and pleasures of this life. I am tempted daily to see work, pleasure, and financial security as more important than you and the blessings you freely give your disciples. Help me, Lord Almighty, to see you clearly. Send your Holy Spirit into my heart to sharpen my spiritual vision as I take these daily walks with you. When I read and ponder your passion, open my eyes to see you beaten and bloody for me. With clear spiritual vision, help me treasure you above all else. Amen.

31

A Cross for Simon

As they led him away, they seized Simon from Cyrene, who was on his way in from the country, and put the cross on him and made him carry it behind Jesus. A large number of people followed him, including women who mourned and wailed for him. Jesus turned and said to them, "Daughters of Jerusalem, do not weep for me; weep for yourselves and for your children. For the time will come when you will say, 'Blessed are the barren women, the wombs that never bore and the breasts that never nursed!' Then 'they will say to the mountains, "Fall on us!" and to the hills, "Cover us!"' For if men do these things when the tree is green, what will happen when it is dry?" (Luke 23:26-31)

The trial was over. Jesus stood condemned by two courts—the Jewish court and the Roman court. The Jewish court had proclaimed Jesus guilty of death twice—once in the dark morning hours and then again in the early morning light of dawn. The Jewish leaders brought Jesus to Pilate's court. Although no evidence supported the condemnation in Pilate's court, the Roman governor issued the order for the crucifixion of the "King of the Jews." Washing his hands of the entire affair, Pilate would never escape what he had done.

As soon as Pilate gave the order, the soldiers took charge of Jesus. They mocked him again as "King of the Jews." Since Jesus could make no appeal and no escape from the judgment of Pilate, why delay the execution? These soldiers quickly took the purple robe off Jesus and put on his own clothes. In an hour or so, they would complete their task of nailing Jesus to the cross. Then they would wait for him to die. Pilate had condemned two others to death. The soldiers simply added Jesus to their grisly agenda. Perhaps Jesus took the place of Barabbas, whom Pilate had released. If that were the case, the soldiers only substituted one condemned man for another—the innocent Jesus for the murderer Barabbas.

In just a few moments, the gates of the Roman fortress opened, and the detail assigned to carry out Pilate's order emerged. Typically, a Roman centurion led the way, riding at the head of the procession. Had we been there, no doubt we would have seen a squad of four soldiers surrounding Jesus with one more soldier carrying a white board with the charge against Jesus written in three languages—Greek, Latin, and Hebrew. Jesus carried his own cross, most likely only the crossbar. The upright portion of the cross was already firmly in the ground, waiting for him. The other two condemned to death that day followed, each one led out in the same way, each one carrying his own cross.

The Romans escorted the procession through the narrow streets of Jerusalem to Calvary. The shops were closed because of the Jewish festival, but a large crowd of people watched and followed. The soldiers tried to keep the procession moving, but it did stop along the way. No one knows if it stopped more than twice, but it certainly stopped at least twice. First, the procession stopped because the Romans forced Simon to carry the cross of Jesus. At the second stop, Jesus talked with the women of Jerusalem, who mourned and wailed the great tragedy of this procession. Only speculation fills in other details not recorded in the gospels.

Simon was on his way into the city. He had come to Jerusalem from Cyrene, a seaport in northern Africa with a substantial Jewish community. Like thousands of other devout Jews, he had come for the Jewish Passover. After eating the Passover with family or friends in Jerusalem, he left the city and spent the night out in the open. In the early hours of Friday, he was headed back into the city. No doubt others who had flocked to Jerusalem for the Passover were beginning to return to the city too. Some returned for the morning offering in the temple, which began at about 9:00 A.M.; others returned to be with family and friends for the opening meal of the Feast of Unleavened Bread, which began at about noon. Whatever the reason, sometime before nine in the morning, Simon's path was blocked by an oncoming procession of condemned men.

Roman imperial power interrupted Simon's plans for the day. Against his will he carried Jesus' cross out of Jerusalem to Calvary. What did this encounter with Jesus mean to Simon? No doubt he shared the experiences of the morning with his wife and his two sons, Alexander and Rufus. Carrying the cross of Jesus did more than alter Simon's plans. It altered his life and the life of his family. The Scriptures record the names of his two sons (Mark 15:21), implying they were well-known when Mark wrote his gospel. One more reference to a Rufus raises some interesting possibilities. The apostle Paul greets a Rufus at the end of his letter to the Romans: "Greet Rufus, chosen in the Lord, and his mother, who has been a mother to me, too" (Romans 16:13). The cross of Christ had claimed new disciples.

I have encountered Jesus too. His cross has changed my life. Although I was by nature dead in my sin and an enemy of God, Jesus has stopped me and made me see the value of his cross. He has chosen me to be his disciple now, in this time and place, just as he has chosen thousands of others to be his disciples. As I take this mental and spiritual journey with him out of Jerusalem to Calvary, I know I must share my Savior with others, especially with the members of my family. I cannot see Jesus crucified and remain unaffected and unchanged. My walk with Jesus continues each day. All believers walk with him every day. He promises to be with us, no matter how heavy our daily crosses.

PRAYER: Lord Jesus, you have stopped me on my way to hell, turned me around, and made me your disciple. You also give me work to do for you as your disciple, and at times you have asked me to suffer because I am your disciple. Both are small crosses to bear for you. I desire to walk with you each day of my life, but I grow weary along the way. May your cross strengthen me to serve you. May your suffering and death for me give me the energy and will to follow you each day. Amen.

32

A Willing Sacrifice

They brought Jesus to the place called Golgotha (which means The Place of the Skull). Then they offered him wine mixed with myrrh, but he did not take it. And they crucified him. Dividing up his clothes, they cast lots to see what each would get. It was the third hour when they crucified him. The written notice of the charge against him read: THE KING OF THE JEWS. *They crucified two robbers with him, one on his right and one on his left.* (Mark 15:22-27)

The procession filed through the gate and out of Jerusalem. It slowly marched up the side of a small hill nearby. There the line of people spread out on the top of Golgotha like ants on top of a mound of sand. Each squad of soldiers took its prisoner to the pole on which he would be crucified. The centurion barked commands to the soldiers, and they obeyed.

They offered each condemned man a drink of wine mixed with myrrh. It was a bitter potion intended to deaden the nerves of those crucified. Why? These Roman veterans had a difficult task to perform. They had to stretch the arms of the prisoner out on the wooden crossbar and hold them still until nails secured them to the wood. They would raise the crossbar up to its position on the pole. Then they would hold the legs of the prisoner still so they could nail them to the cross. No doubt ropes were used to make things easier. Imagine the struggle. It would require brute force to subdue a man who was to be executed. The drink made it easier. Criminals could be managed more easily. The Romans didn't care whether the condemned felt any pain or not. They were only interested in doing their duty—crucifying criminals.

They offered Jesus the same drink, but he refused it. The soldiers would have no trouble with Jesus. He would not struggle to avoid the inevitable. He was a dramatic contrast to the other two executed on the same day. They no doubt cursed the soldiers, spit at them, struggled to avoid the nails, even tried to bite the soldiers, and then screamed terrible cries of anguish as the hammer drove the nails through their hands into the wood. They fought to live. They grasped at a few more seconds of life even in the face of certain death. Jesus was different. He did not need the mind-deadening drink. He laid down his life. He offered no struggle, no curse, no protest.

Only once did he object. When he had stood bound before Annas, he had rebuked the high priest's servant who had struck the first blow of his passion. He had told Peter to stop his wild defense in the garden. He had told the disciples and the others that he could call for 12 legions of angels if he had wanted them. He had answered truthfully to questions posed by Caiaphas and Pilate. He had not met the force of Rome and Judea with equal and opposing force. He willingly embraced his suffering and death.

He showed the full extent of his love for those troubled by sin and death in this world. At about 9:00 A.M., as the sun continued to climb into the morning sky, he stretched out one arm and allowed the soldiers to nail his hand to the cross. Then he stretched out his other arm as the soldiers hammered his other hand to the cross. Finally, after the soldiers lifted the crossbar up and secured it in place, they nailed his feet to the cross. He was crucified—an action by Roman soldiers he did not resist.

Oh, how he loved us! Oh, how he loved me! He willingly began the journey to Jerusalem. He knew clearly what awaited him at his journey's end. He told his disciples exactly what would happen. He did not have to go to Jerusalem, but he went anyways. His goal had all of us clearly in mind. He stretched out his arms and died for us.

We are all trapped in the valley of the shadow of death. We cannot escape death. We are also prisoners of sin, bound by our quest for wealth and power as well as our lust for pleasure. We cannot escape the punishment we deserve, nor can we make up for one angry and bitter word or one evil thought. Only Jesus can release us. He knew there was no other way to wipe away sin and destroy its punishment. By willingly enduring the pain of crucifixion, he rescued us from sin and opened the only way out of the dark valley of pain, misery, and death.

The soldiers had no idea what was happening on Calvary. They played games, ate the meal they brought with them from the garrison, and divided the spoils. But they did note the difference between Jesus and the others. Jesus was a willing victim, crucified between two robbers. The difference would not be lost on the centurion in command. Yet even if Roman soldiers didn't realize it, Jesus was a willing sacrifice for the sins of all the world. Because God loved the world, he gave his son. All those who believe in him will have everlasting life. I believe and I pray God will keep me strong in faith amid all life's hardships that I may receive the reward Jesus has earned for me and all the world.

PRAYER: Without complaint, Lord Jesus, you walked out of Jerusalem to Calvary. Willingly you stretched out your arms so they might nail them to the cross. You thought of me, Lord, and you did it for me. You were lifted up so that I might be forgiven. Fix my eyes on your cross, Lord, so that in good and bad times it may point me to heaven. Amen.

33

Nails, Crown, Cross

So the soldiers took charge of Jesus. Carrying his own cross, he went out to the place of the Skull (which in Aramaic is called Golgotha). Here they crucified him, and with him two others—one on each side and Jesus in the middle. Pilate had a notice prepared and fastened to the cross. It read: JESUS OF NAZARETH, THE KING OF THE JEWS. Many of the Jews read this sign, for the place where Jesus was crucified was near the city, and the sign was written in Aramaic, Latin and Greek. The chief priests of the Jews protested to Pilate, "Do not write 'The King of the Jews,' but that this man claimed to be king of the Jews." Pilate answered, "What I have written, I have written." (John 19:16-22)

The Jews had succeeded. They had resolved to kill Jesus after he had raised Lazarus from the grave. They had concluded that one man had to die in order to preserve the Jewish nation. Their plot had achieved its goal. They had wanted to arrest Jesus in the absence of the great crowd that had greeted him on Palm Sunday. They had received unexpected help from one of Jesus' disciples. Before any crowd could appear to support Jesus, they had stirred up their own crowd to demand his death. The Romans and Pilate had become entangled in the plot, but that meant the Jews hadn't dirtied their hands with a messy execution. The Romans did it. It was almost perfect.

Thursday night after the Passover meal, the Jews and a few Roman soldiers had followed Judas to a quiet garden just outside the walls of Jerusalem. Judas had known Jesus would be there with his disciples; he often went there on his way out of Jerusalem. Armed with swords, clubs, and torches, they had interrupted the prayers of Jesus to arrest him. The crowds the Jewish leaders had feared were gone. The people who had come to celebrate the Passover were gathered with their own families and friends. All over Jerusalem the pilgrims had finished the Passover meal and gone to sleep. In the Garden of Gethsemane, the mob sent to arrest Jesus had bound him and led him through the dark and quiet streets to the palace of Caiaphas.

They had burst into the courtyard of his palace at about 2:00 A.M. While the city slept, Jesus had appeared first before Annas and then before Caiaphas. When the high priest had put Jesus under oath, Jesus had told the truth and confessed that he was Christ, the Son of God. Outraged at the answer of Jesus, Caiaphas had torn his own garments and announced that Jesus was deserving of death. They had no reason to proceed; Jesus had claimed to be the Messiah and the Son of God. The soldiers had abused Jesus and kept him bound until the first light of dawn. When the rooster had announced the first light of day, they brought Jesus again before the Sanhedrin. They had to pass judgment a second time in the light of day in order to make everything official. The hearing had taken all of about 15 minutes. They had convicted him again.

Then they had left the high priest's palace and marched Jesus through the empty streets of Jerusalem to Pilate's court. Those celebrating the Passover in Jerusalem had not risen early the day after the feast. Only a few had noticed the commotion in the streets. The Jewish leaders, however, had planned these events and had gathered a crowd of their own to stand before Pilate and scream for the death of Jesus. Pilate already had been waiting for them. His court had begun at dawn, and the Jews had told him they were bringing Jesus for judgment. By 7:30 or 8:00 A.M., the Jews had Pilate's order for the crucifixion of Jesus.

They had succeeded. No crowd, except the one they stirred up to call for the death of Jesus, had come for the trial. Before the city came to life on the day after the Passover, Jesus had been condemned and led out of the city for execution. Simon had been among those beginning to come back into the city, but by 9:00 A.M. Jesus already was nailed to the cross outside Jerusalem. As far as the Jews were concerned, it was too late for anyone or anything to change the course of events. They could even say that if Jesus were the Messiah, God would not have allowed the Romans to execute him.

It was almost perfect. The only flaw was the placard Pilate had attached to the cross of Jesus. It said, "Jesus of Nazareth, King of the Jews." Perhaps it was Pilate's way of thumbing his nose at the Jews. The Jewish leaders wanted the placard changed. The crowds beginning to return to the city should not think Jesus was the Son of David, King of the Jews. No! Jesus only *claimed* to be king. Besides, what an embarrassment to them and all Jews if the Romans actually had executed the King of the Jews. The placard announced their domination by the Romans. Pilate, it appeared, had the last ironic laugh, and he would not change the sign.

But God's plan was perfect. Jesus was the King of the Jews. He was the Messiah and the Son of God, just as he had confessed before Caiaphas. God had planned these events long before the Jewish leaders were born. The Old Testament prophets wrote of Jesus. Zechariah wrote of Jesus' entry into Jerusalem, "See, your king comes to you, righteous and having salvation, gentle and riding on a donkey" (Zechariah 9:9). Isaiah wrote of him being stricken, smitten, and afflicted (Isaiah 53:4). David wrote of the soldiers dividing his garments (Psalm 22:18). The Old Testament Scriptures are filled with references to these events.

This was God's plan in the Garden of Eden when he promised that Satan would be crushed. The centuries had not changed God's plan. Good Friday brought all his plans to their grand conclusion. God's plan was perfect. Jesus was crucified. The Son of David's throne was a cross outside Jerusalem. Jesus was indeed the King of the Jews. In Greek, Latin, and Aramaic it was so. Everyone could understand at least one of those languages and read the sign. Everyone needs to know that God's plan was perfectly executed, just as he had announced it through the prophets centuries earlier.

PRAYER: Lord God, the centuries could not alter your plan to save the world through your Son, Jesus, the Messiah and King of the Jews. A thousand centuries cannot change what you have done through his cross. May I find comfort in your perfect, unchanging love for me and the forgiveness you give me in Jesus. Amen.

34

Father, Forgive Them

Jesus said, "Father, forgive them, for they do not know what they are doing." And they divided up his clothes by casting lots. (Luke 23:34)

Jesus spoke few words during his passion. He had only responded to the servant of Annas, Caiaphas, Pilate, and the women on the street. In each case his response was short and clear. When the false witnesses had accused him, he remained silent. He had spoken no words before Herod. He had not opened his mouth when the soldiers abused him. Jesus had quietly suffered as they hit him, spit on him, and mocked him. Isaiah had foretold, "He was oppressed and afflicted, yet he did not open his mouth; he was led like a lamb to the slaughter, and as a sheep before her shearers is silent, so he did not open his mouth" (Isaiah 53:7).

The Romans had led Jesus to Calvary through the streets of Jerusalem. Then the soldiers had nailed his hands to the crossbar and raised Jesus up on his cross. Above his head they had attached the placard Pilate had prepared, "Jesus of Nazareth, King of the Jews." As soon as the soldiers had finished nailing Jesus to his cross, they descended like vultures on the clothes Jesus wore, a small booty for their gruesome task. They were there to watch the criminals die. No rescuer would come and take these men down from the crosses. Therefore the condemned no longer needed their clothes. The squad of soldiers made a game of dividing the clothing. The undergarment of Jesus was seamless, woven from top to bottom by some loving hand of a friend. Rather than tear it into four shares, the soldiers cast lots for it. Though stained with blood, it still was a prize for some lucky soldier.

Finally Jesus spoke for the first time at Calvary. His words are absolutely remarkable, as every word he spoke from the cross was remarkable. He broke his silence with words of forgiveness. We might have expected words of anger or curses hurled back at the soldiers and the Jewish leaders. We might have expected to hear angry and bitter words, knowing what we would have done in the same situation. We would have desired to get even and looked for revenge. Jesus forgave.

In Gethsemane Jesus had asked his heavenly Father for another way, another cup, but Jesus could not accomplish his mission any other way. Jesus was resolved that his crucifixion and death was the will of his heavenly Father. The relationship between Father and Son remained strong at Calvary. Jesus prayed to his heavenly Father for the forgiveness of those who had inflicted cruel punishment upon him.

I have walked with Jesus many years. In spirit I have walked with him up to Jerusalem each Lenten season and every time I have read or heard the passion history. I have had to make the pilgrimage to his cross again and again when troubled by sin, doubt, and confusion. The path I have worn to the cross is clear in the wilderness of my perverse heart. Again and again I have walked to Calvary for comfort and strength.

So many events and thoughts bring me to the cross of Jesus. Many times I have walked to Calvary to hear these words: "Father, forgive them, for they do not know what they are doing." I find it difficult to forgive others. When I am wronged, I want to get even. I am hurt by the unkind words of others, and my first reaction is to be just as unkind. When others do things to hurt me, I want to get even. Revenge! My sinful human heart is volatile and erupts at the slightest provocation. So I must walk to Calvary and listen to these words of Jesus: "Father, forgive them."

In our professional lives, we may become the subject of cruel and malicious gossip, and others may attack us openly and secretly, criticize us unjustly, stab us in the back, and oppose us for no other reason than that we are doing our jobs. I know—I've felt it frequently. I must walk back to Calvary and hear the words of Jesus each time. It is impossible to forgive without his words. If he can forgive, so can I.

Whatever others do to me, it is nothing when compared with what Jesus' enemies did to him. Yes, God wants me to protect myself from the harm of evildoers, but within my heart I harbor forgiveness, not bitterness or a desire for revenge. The words of Jesus work that change within.

But I must walk the path to Calvary when I come home from work too. Marriage without forgiveness is a bitter struggle. The injuries spouses inflict on each other are especially painful. But the wounds in marriage can be healed by forgiveness and love. I've found it necessary to walk to Calvary and hear the words of Jesus, "Father, forgive." Because he has forgiven me of all I have done and he can forgive others who have done wrong, I am strengthened to forgive.

Sadly, I have had to walk to Calvary and hear these words when I have worked in God's house too. Christians still have the sinful nature. They are not perfect saints in this life; they are sometimes cruel, insensitive, power hungry, and uncaring. Their words and actions reveal their need for forgiveness. When others wrong me in God's house, I once again walk the path to Calvary and listen: "Father, forgive them."

PRAYER: Heavenly Father, you have forgiven me for all I have done. Every sinful word, thought, and action is cleansed by the blood of Jesus. So often I pray as Jesus taught me, "Forgive us our sins as we forgive those who sin against us," but forgiving others is not easy. Work within my heart that I may willingly and joyfully forgive others. Forgive my spirit of revenge and help me overcome it by drawing me back to the cross of Jesus that I might learn to forgive as he did. Amen.

35

Come Down from the Cross

Those who passed by hurled insults at him, shaking their heads and saying, "You who are going to destroy the temple and build it in three days, save yourself! Come down from the cross, if you are the Son of God!" In the same way the chief priests, the teachers of the law and the elders mocked him. "He saved others," they said, "but he can't save himself! He's the King of Israel! Let him come down now from the cross, and we will believe in him. He trusts in God. Let God rescue him now if he wants him, for he said, 'I am the Son of God.'" In the same way the robbers who were crucified with him also heaped insults on him. (Matthew 27:39-44)

Pilate would not change the placard above Jesus. The chief priests had asked Pilate to change the wording so that it stated only a claim of Jesus, not a fact established in a court of law. Pilate would not change it. It read, "Jesus of Nazareth, King of the Jews." Perhaps Pilate wanted to provoke the Jewish leaders and have the last word on this execution. Jesus' crucifixion and the placard on the cross asserted Roman power over the Jews, and no doubt the sign offended the most zealous of the Jews. But the words represented reality. The Jews were dominated by Rome, and Jesus was the King of the Jews. The Jewish leaders resisted both thoughts.

Jesus had disappointed them. They expected a powerful king who could solve all the problems they imagined. They wanted a king who could feed them. When Jesus had fed the five thousand with five barley loaves and two small fish, the crowd wanted to make him their king (John 6:15). They would have acclaimed him as their king whenever he healed their diseases and made the lame walk. If he had raised an army and fought against the Romans, they would have followed him into battle. But Jesus had no army. As he told Pilate, his servants would have resisted if he were that kind of king. The Jews wanted a king who would make life on earth painless, joyful, peaceful, and without problems. They wanted Jesus to restore paradise on earth, where justice, peace, and honor would be hallmarks of the glorious, perfect state.

They did not want a king of truth and life. Whenever Jesus had reminded them of their sin, they had become incensed. He had told them, "Woe to you, teachers of the law and Pharisees, you hypocrites! You clean the outside of the cup and dish, but inside they are full of greed and self-indulgence. Blind Pharisee! First clean the inside of the cup and dish, and then the outside also will be clean" (Matthew 23:25,26). They had rejected Jesus when he had raised Lazarus from the grave, and then they had plotted not only his death but the death of Lazarus as well. They had objected when he forgave the sins of the lame man let down through the roof. On the previous Monday and Tuesday, they had tried to discredit him as he taught in the temple. Thursday night they had condemned him to death when he said he was the Messiah and the Son of God. Friday they crucified him.

The crucifixion took place just outside the walls of Jerusalem. In the early morning sunshine, Jesus and the others hung on their crosses for public display. That was part of crucifixion too. The Romans wanted everyone to see the result of disobedience and rebellion. These crosses, like so many in the Roman empire, stood like bloody billboards announcing Roman power and law. Many, coming into the city for the morning sacrifice and the Feast of Unleavened Bread, would pass by the crosses and read the sign above Jesus.

Those who rejected Jesus as their king mocked and jeered as they passed by. They did not see beyond the cross, the blood, the nails, the soldiers, and Pilate's sign. It was impossible for them to see an atonement for sin and a heavenly Father offering his Son. They had rejected those things. They saw a helpless man apparently unable to come down from the cross. As so often happens, they all attacked the weak.

"Come down from the cross." Yes, if Jesus had wished to establish an earthly kingdom, he would have come down. Instead, he had come to win forgiveness and open the door of heaven. Because he had come to carry out the plan of his heavenly Father to redeem the world, he did not come down from the cross. The words of these Jews came from hearts and minds that saw a different Jesus than I see. I see the King of truth and life suffering to achieve forgiveness of sins once and for all. They saw an enemy meeting a cruel but certain end. They mocked him and challenged him to come down. I praise him and give thanks that he did not come down from the cross. None of them saw the door of paradise open. I do. Later at least one of those who mocked Jesus also saw beyond and peeked into paradise. But at this time most of them scoffed, taunted, and ridiculed the King of the Jews.

I don't think these Jews were all that different from people today. So many today would follow Jesus if he straightened out the mess we live in here. They want a king and savior who can make earth painless, joyful, peaceful, and without problems. If Jesus or his followers would create an ideal world, where justice, peace, and honor prevail in a perfect state, these people would acclaim him as king. When the words of Jesus accuse humans of greed, immorality, anger, lust, and false hearts, that's too much. So they reject him. Then they mock, ridicule, and jeer the followers of Jesus, who speak of forgiveness and eternal life in heaven. Most still want Jesus to come down from the cross and become a powerful earthly king who will wipe away all problems from the earth. I am content to see Jesus on the cross, wiping away all my sins and opening the door of heaven for me.

PRAYER: Jesus, King of heaven, I praise and thank you for your suffering and death on Calvary. You loved me enough to stay on the cross and complete your work of salvation. When the world mocks me and taunts me because I am your disciple, strengthen my faith by your cross that I may remain faithful to you. Keep my eyes fixed on your cross and the forgiveness and life it brings. Amen.

36

Oh, Judas, No!

When Judas, who had betrayed him, saw that Jesus was con-demned, he was seized with remorse and returned the thirty sil-ver coins to the chief priests and the elders. "I have sinned," he said, "for I have betrayed innocent blood." "What is that to us?" they replied. "That's your responsibility." So Judas threw the money into the temple and left. Then he went away and hanged himself. (Matthew 27:3-5)

When Jesus was crucified at 9:00 A.M. on Friday, it was about seven or eight hours since Judas had greeted Jesus with a kiss in the garden. In the darkness sometime after midnight, Judas had led sol-diers into the garden to arrest Jesus. After the soldiers had bound Jesus and led him to the palace of Caiaphas, the 11 other disciples had fled into the night. John and Peter had stopped, summoned their courage, and cautiously followed the mob. Judas no doubt had stayed at the front of the mob until they arrived at the palace. Per-haps he had collected his 30 pieces of silver when Jesus had been delivered.

From that point on, things happened faster and differently than Judas ever had imagined. Before dawn Jesus was condemned to death for blasphemy. Just after dawn Jesus was turned over to Pilate, who issued the order to crucify him. Jesus was led out of Jerusalem and crucified by 9:00 A.M. Judas must have asked himself what he had done. Did he imagine Jesus would escape as he had before? Did he expect Jesus to come down from the cross? Sometime between the arrest in the garden and the death of Jesus, everything Judas had done came crashing down on him. The words of Jesus predicting his betrayal. The sop in the upper room. The kiss. Jesus' words to him in the garden.

Judas was guilty. He knew it. He was caught in his sin, trapped with no escape, no reasonable explanation, and no excuse. He said so when he came to the chief priests and elders: "I have sinned . . . for I have betrayed innocent blood." He was overcome with deep remorse over the enormity of his action. He couldn't lie about it; too many people had seen him. He couldn't hide until it was all over; his conscience wouldn't let him do that. He couldn't escape to a faraway place because he could not escape the guilt he felt inside. No matter where he went, he would carry the memory of the betrayal with him. Besides, 30 pieces of silver wasn't enough to buy a comfortable escape or a new life in another place.

His greed brought him to despair. Judas was sorry for his sins, but he could not find any solution. The cross reminded him of his betrayal. He did not see forgiveness in the blood of Jesus. Unlike the thief, Judas did not see the gate of paradise open at the cross. He did not believe Jesus could help him. Judas believed he was beyond help. In his mind, God could not help him. He could not wait for the Lord. He could not turn his heavy heart to the Lord. He shut out every Scripture passage he had ever learned, and he slammed the door on the tender words of Jesus before they touched his heart. He had heard Jesus say, "Come to me, all you who are weary and burdened, and I will give you rest" (Matthew 11:28). But his heart did not turn to Jesus.

What a tragedy! Judas chose what seemed like a solution. He threw the coins into the temple and ended his life. But this was not a solution. I think of Judas now and the thoughts that must torment him in hell. He had been very close to Jesus. Judas had heard Jesus' words, seen his miracles, walked and talked with him and the other disciples. The kiss in the garden tortures Judas and will for the rest of eternity. If he could, he would go back, change it all, and rewrite history. But he cannot. He saw only one solution. He did not see the solution Jesus provided—the forgiveness Jesus won on the cross for all people, including Judas.

As disciples of Jesus walk through life, the path is filled with obstacles. Some of them we learn to go around. Others we can crawl over. Still others we cannot solve. When our own mistakes create problems we cannot solve, we suffer remorse and guilt. At times we cannot hide, lie our way out of things, or go back and change history. We are stuck by our sins and shortcomings. Turning away from Jesus and God is not the solution, no matter how deep the pain or insurmountable the problems. Jesus cleanses every sin, even the most heinous. He promises to provide the solution we need at the time we need it.

Repentance is the answer to every disciple's sin. When I think how often I have failed to be a model disciple of Jesus, I am filled with remorse. I cannot take back one angry word. I have often longed to reach out and catch my words before anyone can hear them, but I cannot. Nor can I turn back the clock on one act of selfish ambition or greed. I stand at the cross of Christ as guilty as Judas, but I also know the forgiveness and love of Jesus. No matter how great the sin, the blood of Jesus cleansed it. In faith I cling to his forgiveness and find in it the strength to be a better disciple.

PRAYER: When I feel there is no hope and no help, Lord, rescue me from my feelings of helplessness. Do not let me descend into despair. Work in my heart through your Word that I may find comfort and strength in your love and forgiveness. When all seems dark and I am terrified, reach out your hand of love and pull me from the abyss of my spiritual depression. Then wrap me in the blanket of your care that I may gain strength to go on. Amen.

37

Mother Mary

Near the cross of Jesus stood his mother, his mother's sister, Mary the wife of Clopas, and Mary Magdalene. When Jesus saw his mother there, and the disciple whom he loved standing nearby, he said to his mother, "Dear woman, here is your son," and to the disciple, "Here is your mother." From that time on, this disciple took her into his home. (John 19:25-27)

John watched it all. He had followed the mob from Gethsemane and walked into the high priest's palace unopposed because he was known there. He had followed Jesus to Pilate's court in the early light of morning. When Jesus had been condemned, John followed the detail leading Jesus out of the city to Calvary. He had watched as the soldiers crucified Jesus and the two criminals. Then it seems he had returned to Jerusalem and escorted Mary and the other women to the cross. Perhaps he had a home in Jerusalem where the women had waited for him.

One of the women was John's mother, Salome, Mary's sister. The other two Marys were there too, Mary Magdalene and Mary the wife of Clopas. Some have speculated that Clopas was the brother of Joseph, Jesus' step-father. These women were disciples of Jesus and had cared for his needs during his ministry on earth. They had come up to Jerusalem with him this last time. Their journey led to the cross.

We are not surprised that they wanted to be present at his death. Because John stood there with them, it seems he had brought them to the cross. In some ways it was a grim family gathering to stand the deathwatch. Like thousands of other families throughout the centuries, they drew themselves together around the deathbed of a loved one, waiting for the last breath. What heartache! Their tears and sobbing spilled out of hearts deeply wounded. They were helpless; they could change nothing. They stood near the cross and watched.

Jesus noticed them standing there. When he saw his mother and John, the disciple he loved, he spoke. He said, "Dear woman, here is your son." He addressed her tenderly, but without using her name, and entrusted her into the care of John. He left nothing in doubt when he also addressed John, "Here is your mother." Both Mary and John clearly understood the intent of Jesus. From that moment John took responsibility for Mary. He took her into his home. Perhaps, after the instructions of Jesus, John and Mary left Calvary together, walking silently back to John's home while the other women stayed behind to wait for death to come. After John took Mary home, he walked back to the cross to watch with his mother, Salome, and the other two Marys. Later when death did come to Jesus, they were there, watching from a distance.

My journey up to Jerusalem brings me to the cross too. Through the words of the gospel writers, I can see and hear what took place on Calvary. I can imagine standing with John and the women. All around me the chief priests mock and jeer Jesus on the cross. The soldiers join in too and no doubt drink too much cheap wine while they keep watch at the foot of the three crosses.

When I hear these words of Jesus and see John care for Mary, the mother of Jesus, I am filled with admiration for John. He was there. None of the other disciples are mentioned at the cross, only John, the disciple Jesus loved. I admire John for his quiet courage. He was closest to Jesus in the upper room, and he stayed close to Jesus in spite of the danger.

I also admire him for the love he showed at the cross. *Love* for him was not some empty word. For John, love meant that he would stand with Mary in her hour of need. Love meant compassion for her, even if his own heart was also breaking. Love meant caring for a woman he had come to know and respect.

This touching moment at the cross says even more about Jesus than it does about John or Mary. Jesus demonstrated the meaning of love. He took care of his family to the very end. Mary was without a husband and without anyone to care for her; Joseph had died. Jesus did not abandon his mother to the future. He provided the care she needed. Notice the confidence Jesus had in John. The Lord could have cared for his mother in a thousand other ways, but the care and love of Jesus for his mother came through the human hands of John.

At the cross I learn that love is not a word or feeling. It is an action. Jesus entrusted his mother to John. The disciple Jesus loved took Mary and cared for her in his own home. Jesus has entrusted the care of others to us as his disciples. We are to care for our families and our fellow Christians. I am a disciple of Jesus, and as his disciple, I am to love others. At the cross I learn another lesson about love. Jesus' cross gives me the will to love and the power to act on my desire to love others.

PRAYER: Lord, you have entrusted the members of my family into my care. They are special treasures you ask me to love all my days. Lord, help me love them as you love me. Give me opportunity to show my love by acts of compassion, concern, and caring. Lord, you also bring many others into my life. Fill me with your love so that I might also love them and show compassion for them whenever they face worry, fear, uncertainty, and trouble. May your care of others in this world come through my human heart and hands. Amen.

38

Today, Paradise

One of the criminals who hung there hurled insults at him: "Aren't you the Christ? Save yourself and us!" But the other criminal rebuked him. "Don't you fear God," he said, "since you are under the same sentence? We are punished justly, for we are getting what our deeds deserve. But this man has done nothing wrong." Then he said, "Jesus, remember me when you come into your kingdom." Jesus answered him, "I tell you the truth, today you will be with me in paradise." (Luke 23:39-43)

King of the Jews! All morning long those words brought laughter, sneers, and taunts to Jesus. The soldiers boasted they had crucified the King of the Jews. What a joke that this bloody, condemned man was king. Even his face was puffed and swollen from the beatings he took. Those who had a casual acquaintance with him might not even have recognized him. The chief priests and elders of the Jews made sure everyone understood Pilate's joke. They mocked him and ridiculed him as the Christ, "He saved others . . . but he can't save himself!" (Mark 15:31). Even both criminals joined the loud and rowdy chorus.

The placard nailed above the head of Jesus announced he was indeed "King of the Jews." Yet the soldiers did not fight against those who opposed his execution. When the Romans had led Jesus out of Jerusalem, women mourned his condemnation in the streets. His followers had not ambushed the Roman soldiers in an attempt to rescue their king. Only his family and a few others had come to Calvary, and they quietly watched. Jesus had refused the painkiller offered by the Romans. He had not cursed the soldiers or threatened them. When they had nailed him to the cross, he prayed for their forgiveness. He suffered like a king—with courage and dignity. He was different from the Romans, the chief priests, and the criminals.

He was greater and nobler than any of them. He wore his innocence as the king he was and endured his pain without complaint.

All this made an impression on one of the men crucified with Jesus. When the soldiers first nailed this robber to the cross, he also had mocked Jesus. Both robbers had railed on Jesus. But the Holy Spirit worked in this robber's heart through all he heard and saw. Sometime in the morning hours, this robber changed his mind about Jesus. He stopped insulting Jesus. Then he rebuked the other condemned man, who continued to ridicule Jesus.

The penitent thief understood the kingdom of Jesus. Yes, Jesus was the King of the Jews, but he was not like Caesar, Herod, or even Pilate. From everything the thief's natural eyes could see, Jesus was not a king and had no kingdom. But the Holy Spirit had opened his eyes to see beyond the soldiers, Jewish leaders, and the cross. Jesus was the King of heaven. That's where Jesus came from. He was King above all.

The thief recognized Jesus as his Lord. He was frightened by that at first. This King was innocent, but he was not. He deserved the execution he endured. Jesus did not. The penitent thief knew that greater punishment awaited him after the crucifixion was over. He deserved God's judgment for his deeds after this life was over. The thief acknowledged his guilt and turned to Jesus. Only the King crucified with him could help. He could open the door of heaven. So the man prayed, "Jesus, remember me when you come into your kingdom."

Jesus responded with a promise only the King of heaven could make: "Today you will be with me in paradise." No mere man could issue such a promise. Only the King of the Jews could grant someone a place in his eternal kingdom. In a few hours the three of them would be dead—Jesus first, then the other two. After the suffering of the day, this thief would enter heaven. "Today," Jesus said. No other stops. No delays. Today in paradise. The promise of Jesus was a remarkable comfort for the penitent thief. It helped him endure the last painful hours of his life on earth. When his painful ordeal was over, he would be with Jesus in heaven. In that kingdom God would wipe away every tear from his eyes. "There [would] be no more death or mourning or crying or pain, for the old order of things has passed away" (Revelation 21:4).

In my spiritual journey through life, I find it necessary to walk often to the cross and hear these words of Jesus. What wonderful words they are! I know my guilt before God. I sin daily and deserve nothing but his judgment. But like the thief, I turn to Jesus. At his cross I find rich forgiveness for all my sins. His grace and mercy created faith within me, and I claim Jesus as my King.

My King rules all things, and I must face him someday. But I do not fear, because he grants me forgiveness. I believe that the words he spoke to the thief are for me too. When my life is over, he promises paradise with him. I base my hope on the words of Jesus. He is Lord of lords and King of kings. I do not deserve to live with him in heaven, but by his grace and mercy I will. When death comes to me, that day I will be with Jesus. No other stops. No delays.

I do not know what lies ahead for me before the day I leave this earth, but the promise of Jesus sustains me when I confront life's storms. Jesus has prepared a place for me in his Father's house. He has promised that I shall live there forever after my time on earth is over. By the power of the Holy Spirit, I see the paradise above, no matter how dark the days.

PRAYER: Lord Jesus, remember me when my last hour comes. My sins are great, and I deserve nothing but your judgment, but I turn to you and plead for mercy. You have paid the penalty I deserve and opened the door of paradise for a poor, miserable, wretched, unworthy sinner like me. Lord, make room in your kingdom for me, and sustain my faith through all the pain, sorrow, and misery of life that I may finally come joyfully into paradise and sing your praise. Amen.

39

Forsaken!

At the sixth hour darkness came over the whole land until the ninth hour. And at the ninth hour Jesus cried out in a loud voice, "Eloi, Eloi, lama sabachthani?"—which means, "My God, my God, why have you forsaken me?" When some of those standing near heard this, they said, "Listen, he's calling Elijah." (Mark 15:33-35)

For three hours the condemned men hung from their crosses. The long morning shadows slowly surrendered to the sun as it climbed higher in the sky. The cool early morning hours disappeared. The soldiers, the curious, the Jews, and the few friends of Jesus expected a hot, sunny day. The three men hanging on crosses felt the hot sun bake their naked bodies. As the sun stood overhead at noon, no shadows or shade brought relief on Calvary.

Then at the sixth hour, about noon, something unusual happened. The sun stopped shining, almost as if it disappeared from the sky. Darkness replaced the dazzling bright Judean sun. Unexpectedly the sun shut its eye and became dark. For three hours it was as if the sun took an afternoon nap. Light gave way to darkness, and darkness ruled the day. It could not have been an eclipse because the Passover was celebrated at the time of the full moon. It was an unusual event, an unexplained phenomenon—awesome and ominous.

For three more hours, in the darkness, Jesus hung on the cross and suffered, his body gradually losing its strength. Before he had come to Calvary, he had been weakened by the beatings and needed help to carry his cross out of Jerusalem. He chose to suffer as a human being and refused to draw on the strength and power he had as true God. Like others who died by crucifixion, Jesus—a man crucified, beaten, and bloody—slowly inched toward death. Each breath brought his end closer. Perhaps the sun had closed its eye because it could not watch the Son of Man and Son of God die.

Three hours after the sun grew dark, Jesus spoke again. This time he did not react to those who surrounded his cross. Instead, his words flowed from the great turmoil inside his heart. "My God, my God, why have you forsaken me?" Jesus had descended deep into the profoundest pit of anguish. Twice he called on the name of God, "My God, my God," doubling the depth of his agony and the urgency of his question. God had turned away from him as surely as the sun had refused to shine. God had forsaken his Son.

I cannot fully comprehend what Jesus suffered. Hell is the only place I know where God chooses not to be with his love and care. He withdraws his gracious presence from the damned. They are separated from God and from every blessing of his grace. I have felt abandoned at times. I have felt all alone and imagined that no one cared even a thought about me, but I have never really been alone; someone has always cared about me.

Jesus was deserted by his closest friends, his disciples. Only a few family members came to watch at the cross. His enemies surrounded him and hurled insults at him. Then God forsook him. What agony! I cannot know what it feels like when God abandons someone, withdraws his presence, and chooses to turn away. Wherever I go on earth, God watches over me. He knows the number of hairs on my head and when a sparrow falls from the sky. But to be forsaken by God, abandoned by him, and beyond his care and love is more than I can understand—more than I ever want to experience.

But Jesus was forsaken by God. Yes, God chose to turn away from Jesus. Why? Because Jesus assumed responsibility for the sins of the world. The King of the Jews endured what every sinner deserves. I deserve to be separated from the love, grace, glory, and joy of God. My sins deserve such punishment. The holy, innocent Son of God took my place and suffered what I deserved.

Although these words ring with desperate torment, they are comforting to me. Because of Jesus I will never be abandoned by God. By faith in Jesus I have made his suffering mine. God has accepted the torment of Jesus as a substitute for my own. As long as I cling to Jesus, God will not turn away from me. He will not abandon me. Instead, he will continue to be with me, just as he promised. Only when I think I have no need for Jesus and abandon him will I begin to descend into the deep pit of hell. If I would persist in unbelief and arrogance, God would have no choice but to say, "Depart from me" (Matthew 25:41). Then I would be abandoned by God and sent away from his loving presence forever.

When those who surrounded Jesus heard this cry of anguish, they did not understand. They thought he had called for Elijah. How twisted is the mind of unbelief! What they heard was the Son of God enduring hell for them. They laughed at him. Unbelief always twists and laughs at God's love in Jesus. He was abandoned to hell for them too, but if they persisted in the laughter of unbelief, they themselves would be forsaken by God.

PRAYER: How often, heavenly Father, do I think you have abandoned me! When all I do seems in vain, when friends desert me, when I am ridiculed, or when I fail miserably, I am dejected and feel alone and abandoned. At those times, Lord, let me hear the words of Jesus, "My God, my God, why have you forsaken me?" He was abandoned so that I will never be abandoned. He was rejected because of my sin so that you might embrace me with forgiveness and love. Because you abandoned Jesus, you have promised me, "I will never leave you or forsake you." In my darkest hours, may your presence cheer me and give me hope. Amen.

40

Thirsty

Later, knowing that all was now completed, and so that the Scripture would be fulfilled, Jesus said, "I am thirsty." A jar of wine vinegar was there, so they soaked a sponge in it, put the sponge on a stalk of the hyssop plant, and lifted it to Jesus' lips. (John 19:28,29)

John may have returned to Calvary after taking Mary to his home in time to hear these words. He alone recorded them, and he included nothing in his gospel between the time Jesus entrusted Mary to his care and these words. His word "later" could mark the time when he returned to Calvary. He joined the women, who had moved some distance from the cross, and heard these last words of Jesus.

Jesus was thirsty. He had felt the growing heat of the morning sun. Then when the sun grew dark, he continued to suffer for three more hours. Death was near. Thirst is part of almost every human death. I've been in hospital rooms with patients near death and seen their lips parched and their tongues dry as sandpaper. I've watched nurses and family moisten a clean cloth and give it to a patient so he or she could slowly suck the moisture from it. Thirst was a usual occurrence at crucifixion. Jesus is human like all of us and felt what all other humans felt. He was thirsty.

The soldiers kept a jar of vinegar nearby to relieve their own thirst. Thirst came quickly in the hot, dry air of Jerusalem. One of them soaked a sponge with vinegar and lifted it on a stick to Jesus. Perhaps he was one who began to see Jesus as the innocent Lamb of God. The others challenged him and wondered why he would offer this final act of kindness. They said, "Leave him alone. Let's see if Elijah comes to save him" (Matthew 27:49). No kindness lived in the hearts of most of these hardened veterans. They still could not make any sense of the anguished cry of Jesus, *"Eloi, Eloi, lama sabachthani?"* To them it was a cry for Elijah.

Jesus sucked the vinegar from the sponge and found relief from his thirst. The final drink of the King of the Jews was vinegar, not expensive wine. The poor used vinegar to satisfy their thirst; so did Jesus. He was crucified as a common criminal and had no throne but the cross. His final banquet was nothing but vinegar. This King of the Jews had been born in a stable, had ridden into Jerusalem on a donkey, had only the clothes on his back, and had received vinegar to drink. Yet from this lowly stump of Jesse's royal line came unsurpassed blessings for all the world.

John noted that these words fulfilled the Scripture. When Jesus cried out, "My God, my God, why have you forsaken me?" the soldiers did not understand. John and the other disciples knew those were the first words of Psalm 22, which clearly described the events on Calvary centuries before they occurred. The psalm foretold the mockery and the insults. It foretold the soldiers casting lots for the clothing of Jesus, and it described his thirst, "My strength is dried up like a potsherd, and my tongue sticks to the roof of my mouth; you lay me in the dust of death" (verse 15). Another psalm even identified the vinegar, "They put gall in my food and gave me vinegar for my thirst" (69:21).

The events outside Jerusalem on Calvary did not happen by chance. God had planned all these events centuries before they occurred. God carefully had considered all the details and foretold many of them through his Old Testament prophets. Old Testament believers had longed to see the fulfillment of the prophecies. Even the prophets went back and searched their own writings when the Holy Spirit had predicted the sufferings of Christ through them (1 Peter 1:10,11).

I marvel at the plan of God. When Adam and Eve disobeyed, God could have destroyed his creation and started all over again. But he chose to rescue Adam and Eve and all who followed them. He promised that a Savior would come and undo the work of the serpent. Over the centuries God revealed more and more details about that promise. Finally those details ended at the cross of Calvary. The trip up to Jerusalem did not start at Ephraim. The road stretched back to Eden and God's first promise of a Savior from sin.

The Old Testament Scriptures recorded the events that were important along the way to Calvary through the centuries before Christ. Those words pointed the millions of Old Testament believers ahead to this moment on Calvary. Jesus knew all was completed, and he finally fulfilled the last little detail when he asked for relief from his thirst. The writers of the Old Testament had told of these events before they occurred. The writers of the New Testament recorded the history of these events and their meaning for us after they had taken place. All the writers were inspired by the Holy Spirit to record things as God wanted them recorded. "Prophecy never had its origin in the will of man, but men spoke from God as they were carried along by the Holy Spirit" (2 Peter 1:21).

No one can understand the Scriptures without understanding the great plan of God. If you do not understand Calvary and the crucifixion of Jesus for the sins of the world, the Scriptures will forever be an obscure and dark book. Christ is the message of the Bible from beginning to end.

PRAYER: How precious, O Lord, is the Scripture given to me and all the world by inspiration of the Holy Spirit. When I am confused by some passage, Lord, may I remember that you gave your Book so I might know Jesus and understand the meaning of his suffering and death. May I read, note, and learn the message of Christ's death again and again so that my faith may be strengthened. Amen.

41

Finished!

When he had received the drink, Jesus said, "It is finished."
(John 19:30)

The final words of Jesus pile up at the end of his suffering. Four of the seven words of Jesus from the cross come within just a few moments. About 3:00 P.M., the ninth hour, Jesus called out from the depth of his agony, "My God, my God, why have you forsaken me?" Just a few moments later, he moaned, "I am thirsty." When one man lifted a soaked sponge up to his lips, Jesus sucked the vinegar from the sponge. Then without any delay, he announced, "It is finished." Perhaps at this moment the darkness began to lift. It had been dark since noon, but at the ninth hour the darkness crept away and the sunlight once more returned.

But was the trip up to Jerusalem finished? Jesus had come to Jerusalem knowing everything that had happened in the last 18 hours would take place. We can trace his steps to the upper room with his disciples, to the garden, then before the Jewish and Roman courts, and finally out of Jerusalem to Calvary. Jesus knew it all beforehand, and he had announced it to his disciples on more than one occasion. Yet on those occasions he had also told them he would rise from the dead on the third day. So Jesus had one more step to take.

What was finished then? His pain and misery were almost over and would come to an end in just a few moments. But there was something more important that was finished. Jesus had offered the perfect sacrifice for the sins of the world. The Scriptures tell us the suffering of Jesus was enough to pay for the sins of all people. "He has appeared once for all at the end of the ages to do away with sin by the sacrifice of himself" (Hebrews 9:26). Jesus announced the completion of that one sacrifice for sin. It's done!

All the words of Jesus from the cross are precious, but none is more precious than this simple sentence, "It is finished." I treasure that sentence because it assures me that my sins have been paid for completely. Because Jesus suffered and finished his work, God does not count my sins against me. My sins are punished already. It's all done and finished. That's what Jesus' announcement means. I am justified before God; I am acceptable to him because Jesus suffered what I deserved. He took all my sins and gives me his perfect, holy, and righteous life. His life became mine; mine became his.

The sacrifice of Jesus is complete not just for me but also for all the world. Even the worst sins are already paid for and washed away. Jesus paid for the betrayal and suicide of Judas and for the world's most horrible criminals as surely as he paid for my sins. The sacrifice of Jesus does not exclude any sinner; no sin is too great to be washed away by his blood. So the Bible clearly tells us, "God was reconciling the world to himself in Christ, not counting men's sins against them" (2 Corinthians 5:19). John, who stood at the cross and heard these words, later wrote, "[Christ] is the atoning sacrifice for our sins, and not only for ours but also for the sins of the whole world" (1 John 2:2). It is finished for all the world!

Jesus did it all. No human needs to complete or finish what he has done. The removal of all sins is a gift from God to all the world. It's like the morning sunrise; the sun comes up every morning, no matter what I do, think, or feel. The work of Jesus is finished just as surely. It's done, no matter what I think, feel, say, or do. Even faith in Jesus does not finish the sacrifice for sin or complete it. It is finished! Faith only receives the free, perfect, and complete gift of God. Repentance does not add to it either. When people repent, they turn away from the sin in their lives and accept the completed gift of God by faith. The removal of all sin and the declaration that all the world is free from sin are accomplished facts. Jesus said so: "It is finished."

With these words of Jesus, God announces that he will not pass judgment upon human beings on the basis of sin. Sin has been removed. But God will pass judgment upon human beings on the basis of what they do with this unconditional gift of forgiveness. He says, "Whoever believes and is baptized will be saved, but whoever does not believe will be condemned" (Mark 16:16). Jesus told Nicodemus, "God so loved the world that he gave his one and only Son, that whoever believes in him shall not perish but have eternal life" (John 3:16).

When I make the spiritual journey up to Jerusalem, I come to renew my faith in the completed gift of God. My devotion refreshes my spirit every time I hear that Jesus has paid for my sins. That completed sacrifice for my sins is a power that changes me. First, it has made me a disciple of Jesus. Now I am still imperfect and sin every day, but I can make this pilgrimage up to Jerusalem and find comfort in the sacrifice of Jesus for my sins. Through the power of his forgiveness, I can repent daily. I can turn away from the sin in my life, trust in the forgiveness Jesus died to accomplish, and find the energy in his forgiveness to love Jesus and serve him. When I fail, I return to the cross for reassurance and strength to do better. In any case, it's all finished for me, and I live by that powerful principle.

PRAYER: Lord, draw me back to your cross again and again. Reassure me that I am forgiven by your complete and perfect sacrifice for the sins of the whole world, including my sin. When I am troubled by my sins and doubt, let me hear your words "It is finished." Often I want to do something to earn your love and forgiveness. Teach me, Lord, that I cannot earn the gift you have completed with your suffering on Calvary. Then fill me with gratitude and thanks for your gift of grace. Amen.

42

A Loud Voice

Jesus called out with a loud voice, "Father, into your hands I commit my spirit." When he said this, he breathed his last. The centurion, seeing what had happened, praised God and said, "Surely this was a righteous man." When all the people who had gathered to witness this sight saw what took place, they beat their breasts and went away. But all those who knew him, including the women who had followed him from Galilee, stood at a distance, watching these things. (Luke 23:46-49)

Death comes to crucified, condemned criminals slowly. It creeps into the chest and takes energy and life little by little. At first the two criminals joined the crowd in hurling insults at Jesus. Then one turned to Jesus with words of repentance. Six hours later both criminals were quiet; they had no energy to speak. What little energy they had left was spent on breathing. Death had crept inside them both and relentlessly continued to squeeze the life out of their bodies.

Jesus hung there with them, but he spoke four times in the last moments of life. Death had to wait until Jesus was ready, like a dog waiting for a scrap from its master's table. Death could not begin slowly to crowd life from his heart and mind. Jesus was innocent and holy. He was not subject to death. The earlier words of Jesus in this ninth hour had been loud and clear enough for the soldiers to understand. They had mocked him for calling Elijah, and one of them had satisfied the Savior's thirst by raising a sponge dripping with vinegar to his lips. Then, "It is finished." Finally Jesus called out with a loud voice, "Father, into your hands I commit my spirit." Jesus gave his body and mind to death. He laid down his life; death did not force it from him. He summoned death, and it came at his call, but not before he called.

The loud voice of Jesus at the end ran counter to what the soldiers expected. They had seen crucifixions before, and criminals gasped for breath at the end. For others, the interval between breaths grew until the condemned finally did not have enough energy to draw another breath. They died with a whimper and a whisper. When Jesus died, he died with a loud cry.

Several other events occurred when Jesus died. They were all extraordinary. The earth shook and rocks split. Even the soldiers felt the quake. The centurion praised God and echoed Pilate's opinion of Jesus: "Surely this was a righteous man." The apostle John and the women watched at some distance. The chief priests and elders had long gone back to Jerusalem to celebrate the Feast of Unleavened Bread, which began at noon. During the last three hours the crowd had thinned, and besides the soldiers, it seems, only those touched by the ministry of Jesus remained. Those who remained to the end wondered what it all meant. They went away in silence and sorrow.

The other events took place in different parts of the city. Some of the tombs of God's people broke open, and their bodies were raised to life. When Jesus arose, they went into Jerusalem and appeared to many. In Jerusalem the curtain of the temple was torn in two from top to bottom. That curtain separated the part of the temple that represented the presence of the holy God of Israel from the rest of the temple. The high priest entered the Most Holy Place only once a year, on the Day of Atonement. When Jesus died, sin no longer separated human beings from God. The atonement had been completed once and for all. No other sacrifices are ever needed. Jesus paid for the sins of all the world.

These final words of Jesus have encouraged Christians throughout the centuries. Death holds no terror for those who believe. Death obeyed the voice of Jesus, and believers in Jesus need not fear death. Jesus confronted death with the confidence that his heavenly Father would keep him safe after his last breath. He committed his spirit to his Father as any of us would commit a valuable possession for safekeeping to someone we trust.

Like the women, I have stood, in spirit, at the cross of Jesus. I have read the words of Jesus many times. I have heard Lenten sermons based on these words. Considering all that Jesus did on the cross, I am ready to entrust my spirit to my heavenly Father as Jesus did. Jesus told me that I have a place in paradise waiting for me. He completely paid for my sins. As I go through life, I do not know when my last hour shall come. Death may creep into my body and slowly squeeze life from it. On the other hand, it may come swiftly and crush the breath from me. I leave that up to God's will. When he calls me to come home to him, I can confidently entrust my spirit into his hands.

My journey up to Jerusalem always gives me more than I imagine. Each time I come, I find a Savior who loved me enough to lay down his life for me. Each time I stand at his cross, I hear again that my sins have been paid in full for all time. Each time I hear the loud voice of Jesus, I am encouraged to confront death with confidence and pray as he did: "Father, into your hands I commit my spirit."

PRAYER: Even death, Lord Jesus, must wait for your call. These last words are words of triumph and hope. When I am troubled by death, may I find comfort in these words. When I am fearful of what awaits me after death, strengthen my faith that I might entrust my soul into your powerful and loving hands. Each day, fill me with confidence that I may not live my days here in fear of death but in the joy of the life to come. Amen.

43

Broken Legs

Now it was the day of Preparation, and the next day was to be a special Sabbath. Because the Jews did not want the bodies left on the crosses during the Sabbath, they asked Pilate to have the legs broken and the bodies taken down. The soldiers therefore came and broke the legs of the first man who had been crucified with Jesus, and then those of the other. But when they came to Jesus and found that he was already dead, they did not break his legs. Instead, one of the soldiers pierced Jesus' side with a spear, bringing a sudden flow of blood and water. The man who saw it has given testimony, and his testimony is true. He knows that he tells the truth, and he testifies so that you also may believe. (John 19:31-35)

At 9:00 A.M. the Roman soldiers had mocked Jesus, but at 3:00 P.M. some of them changed their minds about the "King of the Jews." Jesus was different. He was not a typical, hardened, coarse criminal. He forgave. He took care of his mother. He was innocent. He endured the pain and the verbal abuse. Then the sun grew dark at noon. When Jesus died, the earthquake terrified them. Watching Jesus die had left its mark on them. After all this the centurion acknowledged Jesus as a righteous man and the Son of God. The friends of Jesus, mostly women, watched in sorrow as he died before their eyes. Others who watched until the end went home shaking their heads and beating their breasts.

If the others had been affected by the death of Jesus, the Jewish leaders remained unaffected. They showed no remorse for what they had done. Early in the day, they had refused to enter Pilate's court because they did not want to be defiled by contact with anything ceremonially unclean in a Gentile's house. Pilate had come out to them. Once Jesus was crucified, they had come to the cross and ridiculed him. They had made it clear that the placard Pilate had tacked above Jesus was just a joke. Then at about noon they had celebrated the opening meal of the Feast of Unleavened Bread, a feast of great joy, in the darkness at home with their families.

It was three in the afternoon when Jesus died. For the Jewish leaders, this was a time of celebration. They had considered Jesus a threat because he had raised Lazarus from the dead. Only a few weeks earlier that miracle had pushed them to plot the death of Jesus. The carpenter from Galilee was dead. Their plan to kill him had succeeded. They believed that their lives would go on as they had before Jesus came.

The sunset on this Friday marked the beginning of the Sabbath, as it did every Sabbath Day before. Of course, this Sabbath, because it occurred during the Feast of Unleavened Bread, was special. The Jewish leaders wanted to ensure that everything was just right for the Sabbath, and they wanted to follow every precept of Scripture. The law God gave Moses said clearly: "If a man guilty of a capital offense is put to death and his body is hung on a tree, you must not leave his body on the tree overnight. Be sure to bury him that same day, because anyone who is hung on a tree is under God's curse. You must not desecrate the land the LORD your God is giving you as an inheritance" (Deuteronomy 21:22,23).

These criminals had to be removed from their crosses. The Law of Moses required no less. So the Jewish leaders petitioned Pilate to take steps to bring these executions to an end before sunset. The Romans knew how to do it. They would speed death by breaking the legs of the criminals. It was painful and brutal. With a large club or mallet, the soldiers would bash the legs of the criminals on the crosses. Without the support of their legs, whatever breath was left in the condemned men would soon disappear, and death would come. If there was any further delay, the soldiers would pierce the criminal's chest cavity with a spear to make sure he was dead.

The Roman detail carried out its grisly orders. John and the women no doubt watched as the Romans broke the legs of one of the men crucified with Jesus and then the legs of the other. The soldiers knew Jesus was already dead. Breaking his legs would not inflict more pain nor would it speed death. So why should they do it? Instead of breaking his legs, the soldier pierced his side with a spear, which penetrated his heart and lungs. Blood and water flowed from his side, perhaps the blood and clear fluid in the sac surrounding his heart. Jesus was dead. Their orders had been carried out. Pilate was satisfied, and so were the Jews.

It is hard for me to think of these broken legs without a mental gasp. What a brutal, painful ordeal for any human, even a hardened criminal! Crucifixion was not some genteel, humane way to end life. It was cruel and unusual punishment, and the broken legs of the criminals only verifies this. Jesus suffered a painful and cruel death meant to humiliate condemned criminals and traitors.

Once again I thank God for what Jesus endured for me. I deserved every brutal pain because I am a sinner, but Jesus suffered it for me. My sins are forgiven. I am amazed that God would suffer for me. Each time I come to the cross and note the events at Calvary, I marvel again at the depth of God's love for sinners. It's enough to take my breath away and bring tears to my eyes. My spiritual journey up to Jerusalem helps me understand "how wide and long and high and deep is the love of Christ" (Ephesians 3:18). I pray I will never tire of learning of that love.

PRAYER: Dear Jesus, your love surpasses anything I have ever known. It is greater than I deserve and greater than I can imagine or comprehend. Draw me to your cross that I may drink at the river of your love and find strength and comfort for my daily life. When my sins drive me to the desert of fear and anguish and dry up my soul, show me the way back to the cross so that I may drink again of your love and be refreshed. Amen.

44

Burial Quiet

Now there was a man named Joseph, a member of the Council, a good and upright man, who had not consented to their decision and action. He came from the Judean town of Arimathea and he was waiting for the kingdom of God. Going to Pilate, he asked for Jesus' body. Then he took it down, wrapped it in linen cloth and placed it in a tomb cut in the rock, one in which no one had yet been laid. It was Preparation Day, and the Sabbath was about to begin. The women who had come with Jesus from Galilee followed Joseph and saw the tomb and how his body was laid in it. Then they went home and prepared spices and perfumes. But they rested on the Sabbath in obedience to the commandment. (Luke 23:50-56)

One last walk with Jesus! One last procession! The friends of Jesus carried his dead body from Calvary to its resting place in the tomb of Joseph. The tomb was nearby, so the walk was not far. I imagine the walk was a quiet one. No one spoke. Each one kept his or her thoughts inside. Grief would not let words escape the heart. If it happened differently and sound filled the air, it probably would have been the wails of grief and sorrow customary at Jewish funerals. The house of Jairus was filled with such wails and so was the house of Mary and Martha in Bethany when Lazarus died. I know that it was not the last walk with Jesus. He rose! But the disciples of Jesus did not fully understand his suffering and did not grasp the hope of resurrection yet. For them the few hours before sunset on Friday were the last of a difficult 18 hours.

According to Roman custom, the judge had the authority to dispose of the bodies of those executed. One man came to Pilate with a request to bury Jesus. He was a high-ranking Jew and had remained quiet during the trial of Jesus. Joseph was a secret disciple until the moment he approached Pilate for the body of Jesus.

Nicodemus, another secret disciple, joined Joseph at Calvary to take Jesus down from the cross. Perhaps he purchased about 75 pounds of myrrh and aloes while Joseph went to ask for Jesus' body. Both men broke their silence about Jesus. They dared to oppose the high priest and the others who plotted his death. They found the courage to come forward and rescue his body from Roman imperial policy. In the process they rescued themselves from fear and secret discipleship.

Both men were wealthy and high-profile leaders in Jerusalem. They concluded that Jesus deserved at least a burial as a wealthy and honored leader. The myrrh and aloes were a generous and loving gift to the Lord they finally openly confessed. Together with those who attended them, they lowered the cross and laid it on the ground. Then they drew out the nails, untied the ropes, and lifted the body from the cross to a stretcher of some kind. They wrapped the body in a clean linen cloth and carried it to Joseph's new tomb. None of the apostles appeared to help. Joseph and Nicodemus led the procession, perhaps with servants they had brought to assist them. The women followed.

The procession hurried to the tomb. The Sabbath began at sunset, and they had to be finished by then. Pilate had ordered the soldiers to break the legs of the condemned men and speed their deaths perhaps at 3:30 or 4:00 P.M. Joseph may have stood before Pilate with his request at 4:30. Quickly he went to Calvary, met Nicodemus, removed the body, and carried it away for burial. They may have arrived at the tomb by 5:30 or even a little later.

In the dwindling light, they brought Jesus inside the tomb. It was dark there, and they may have lit lamps to see. A small space, perhaps nine feet square, just inside the tomb, gave Joseph and Nicodemus room to finish whatever they could before sunset. When they had finished, they set the body on a ledge cut out of the rock on a wall of the tomb. The women watched and noted how and where they laid the body. Nicodemus and Joseph sprinkled a portion of the myrrh and aloes in the grave and reverently left the body inside. The sun had grown red as it descended to the western horizon. One thing remained to be done. They rolled a stone over the entrance to prevent animals from disturbing the body.

I imagine them stepping back after they rolled the stone in place, brushing their hands to remove the dirt, and then pausing just a moment to look at the stone blocking the entrance. Did they sigh? Did tears fill their eyes? I can only imagine their sorrow and grief. The pause in the garden may have lasted longer as they stood before the tomb quietly absorbed in their own thoughts. I have stood long moments at the grave of a dear young friend, silent, mute, awkward, and too filled with questions to do anything but let the tears roll down my cheeks. So I see myself with these disciples at the grave of Jesus.

They did not yet understand the resurrection. They could not yet anticipate it. What could any of them say at such a moment? Jesus was dead. They laid his body to rest. In the growing darkness perhaps they embraced each other before leaving. The women went home with the plan to meet again early Sunday morning and finish the task of embalming the body. When they came back to Jerusalem, it was too late to buy the spices they needed. The shops were all closed for the Sabbath. They would have to wait until after sunset Saturday to buy the spices. All was quiet, and they returned home with their own thoughts.

PRAYER: Lord, your grave was only a temporary resting place. Someday my body will be carried to a resting place too. My spouse, children, grandchildren, and friends will follow in quiet procession. When I am laid to rest, may it be evident that I am a disciple of Jesus. Tears and sorrow will come to those left behind, but like Jesus, I will only be asleep, waiting for you to awaken me on the Last Day. Lord, comfort me whenever I face the end of my life. May I find in your quiet burial the hope of resurrection and the comfort of life forever with you. Amen.

45

Graveside Vigil

The next day, the one after Preparation Day, the chief priests and the Pharisees went to Pilate. "Sir," they said, "we remember that while he was still alive that deceiver said, 'After three days I will rise again.' So give the order for the tomb to be made secure until the third day. Otherwise, his disciples may come and steal the body and tell the people that he has been raised from the dead. This last deception will be worse than the first." "Take a guard," Pilate answered. "Go, make the tomb as secure as you know how." So they went and made the tomb secure by putting a seal on the stone and posting the guard. (Matthew 27:62-66)

The disciples of Jesus observed the Sabbath rest, doing no work from sunset on Friday to sunset on Saturday. The women waited to buy spices. The disciples gathered in secret behind closed and locked doors. The Jewish leaders carefully observed the letter of the law too during these events. They had refused to enter Pilate's court to avoid defilement, and they had petitioned Pilate to remove the bodies of the executed men so that their law would be kept. The Jewish leaders had kept the letter of the law but had violated its essence by screaming for the death of an innocent man.

They justified their sin by claiming that one man should die so that the Jewish nation could survive the Roman occupation. In their minds, the ideas of Jesus threatened to overturn the laws of Moses and the traditions of the elders. They concluded that the more popular Jesus became, the less likely people would continue to observe Jewish customs. If people should follow after Jesus and abandon their Jewish identity and culture, Rome would treat them just like any other conquered nation. They had fought to keep Rome sensitive to the Jewish state and its special and unusual character, including festivals such as Passover. The raising of Lazarus was the last straw for them. For the high priest and his party, one man—Jesus—must die for the sake of the Jewish nation. They justified the execution of Jesus because it was done to ensure the position of the Jewish state in the Roman empire.

When the Sabbath came, the Jewish leaders observed the regulations of the Sabbath laws with a sigh of relief. The threat to their way of life was over. Jesus was dead. But they were concerned that the threat might still have some life. What if the disciples of Jesus would steal his body and claim he rose again from the dead? The words of Jesus had not gone unheard; they just refused to believe them. They thought it best to prevent the return of any possible threat, even if it was only from the frightened and scattered group of Jesus' disciples.

So they sought to preserve their nation and their religion. The chief priests and the Pharisees went to Pilate and asked to make the tomb secure until the threat was over. Three days should be enough since Jesus told the people he would rise on the third day. If they could make sure that Jesus stayed dead longer than three days, they would be able to expose him as the deceiver they believed he was. Jewish laws and regulations would be safe, and the Jewish nation would be secure.

Pilate must have thought the request a bit unusual. Perhaps the request brought a smile to his face. These Jews were still worried about a beaten, ridiculed, and dead "King of the Jews." So Pilate saw no threat. A guard at the tomb of an executed man would humor them; refusal would only antagonize them. Pilate gave the order. The Jews set the guard and sealed the tomb. They believed they had put an end to the threat of Jesus.

They came to Pilate on the Sabbath. What they did violated the Sabbath regulation for rest. Orthodox Jews even today cannot sign their name on the Sabbath because that may be a form of work. Setting a guard and sealing the tomb was work done. No doubt they excused the violation in the same way they excused the execution of Jesus. Their intent was to preserve the Jewish regulations, sacrifices, and laws from erosion by a sect of disciples who followed the deceiver from Galilee, as they called him.

What folly this all was! This Sabbath, as the body of Jesus rested in the grave, was the last Sabbath. No other Sabbath would ever be needed again. All the Jewish laws and regulations that pointed to the coming of Jesus were done. No other sacrifice for sin would ever be needed. No Passover lamb need ever be slaughtered again. The Jewish leaders could not change what God had done nor could they stop what God was about to do.

The seal on the outside of the tomb did nothing to prevent the resurrection of Jesus. In less than 24 hours, the guards would desert their post, and the stone would be rolled away for all the world to see inside. In the wake of the resurrection, thousands of Jews would come to faith and see in the crucified and risen Jesus the fulfillment of all the Old Testament laws and ceremonies. Gentiles too would follow Jesus, and they would never need to observe Passover or the Sabbath regulations. Nothing could stop that. Only stubborn unbelief would refuse to believe what Jesus had done and defiantly cling to ceremonies that had been rendered obsolete by the resurrection of Jesus.

PRAYER: O Holy Spirit, open the eyes of all who do not see the great victory over sin and death that Jesus has accomplished for all the world. Challenge those who blindly follow the opinions of men or the traditions of false religions. May they come to see the folly of every ritual and ceremony that seeks to earn forgiveness or peace. May they find forgiveness and peace where you have provided them—in the suffering, death, and resurrection of Jesus. Amen.

46

Jewish Unbelief

*"Sir," they said, "we remember that while he was still alive
that deceiver said, 'After three days I will rise again.'"*
(Matthew 27:63)

I find it difficult at times to understand how the Jewish leaders
could remain opposed to Jesus and persist in unbelief. The same
things they saw bring comfort and strength to me. I need to take the
spiritual journey up to Jerusalem and see the cross of my Savior often.

On Monday and Tuesday of Holy Week, Jesus had sat in the temple and taught. I see and hear his words much differently than the
Jewish leaders. They sought to trick Jesus into saying something
wrong; I treasure the lessons because they come from God. When
Jesus went to Bethany and called Lazarus from the grave, I see nothing but pure comfort and hope. Jesus is the Resurrection and the
Life. The Jewish leaders had been convinced after the miracle that
Jesus should die and so should Lazarus. They wanted to undo the
work of Jesus; I want to cling to it in faith.

I always wonder how the Jews could be unaffected by the crucifixion of Jesus. They knew Jesus had done nothing wrong. They
trumped up the charges against him, and then they watched as he
was brutally scourged and crucified. After he had been nailed to the
cross and they had finished their mocking, they attended the feast
of joy, ate with their families, and went about their daily tasks. They
celebrated the Sabbath as if nothing out of the ordinary had happened. The temple curtain was torn in two from top to bottom, a
three-hour darkness had interrupted Friday, and an earthquake
shook Jerusalem. Yet they remained firm in their opposition to Jesus
and refused to believe in him. It is as Jesus had said: "How often I
have longed to gather your children together, as a hen gathers her
chicks under her wings, but you were not willing" (Matthew 23:37).

I have encountered unbelief in the hearts of people I've met. Some don't want to be bothered with thinking about Jesus and his crucifixion. They stay busy and active so they don't have time to think of sin and death. As long as they can imagine they are happy, they feel they don't need to believe in Jesus. Others shut Jesus out of their hearts and lives. No matter how clearly the message of Jesus comes to them, they remain blind and dead to the value of the crucifixion and resurrection. They may believe something else—even some other religion—and nothing penetrates their unbelief. Like the Jewish leaders, they turn away from Jesus and go about their daily tasks without him.

When I look inside my own heart, I find the same stubborn rebellion against God. I'm not that much different from the Jewish leaders. By nature I am also blind to the grace of God and dead in my own sins. Nothing I can do will change that, but God has changed me. He opened my eyes and created spiritual life in my otherwise blind and dead heart. He has changed my heart of stone to a heart that beats with faith and love for Jesus. I know thousands whom God has so changed. They treasure Jesus and what he has done.

How did this happen? It is a miracle. The Holy Spirit made this miracle happen through the gospel. He has not promised to work in any other way. He hasn't promised to strike my heart with lightning to make me a believer. He hasn't promised to deepen my faith except when I hear or read the gospel, receive Holy Communion, or remember the message of God's love in Jesus. No believer ever contributes anything, even a decision, to his or her own conversion. The miracle of faith is all God's doing, and the Holy Spirit simply does his work through the message of Jesus. But like the Jewish leaders, we can refuse the miracle of God, and in spite of all the clearest witnesses, we can remain rebellious, spiritually dead, and blind to the grace of God.

If I stay away from Jesus and his Word, I have no promise from God that my faith will survive. As a matter of fact, I have seen what happens when people stay away from God's Word. They move farther and farther away from Jesus and believe that they can get along without him. It has happened again and again. Like the Jewish leaders, they think they can have true religion without Jesus. Such is the perversion of the human heart.

So it's clear why I must take this spiritual journey to Jerusalem regularly. As I read of Jesus' passion, the Holy Spirit works in my heart. He draws me closer to Jesus and deepens my faith. I can only become a better disciple of Jesus when I read, note, and digest the Bible's message of Jesus. The gospel is my lifeline, like the water all plants need to live. Without it I grow weary and weak. Through the gospel the Holy Spirit keeps me walking with Jesus. Each day as his disciple, I take another step. I can only stay on the road if I continue to read and remember all that Jesus has done for me.

PRAYER: Dear Jesus, you have not left me to drift as your disciple. Instead, you have given me the gospel to anchor me against the storms of life, the unbelief of the world around me, and the fears and doubts that arise within me. Lord Jesus, strengthen my battered faith through your Word and sacrament. Let your Word make me a better disciple, one more committed to you and stronger in faith. Do not allow me ever to be unaffected by your passion. May it always strengthen and sustain me so that I may remain your disciple. Amen.

47

He's Risen!

When the Sabbath was over, Mary Magdalene, Mary the mother of James, and Salome bought spices so that they might go to anoint Jesus' body. Very early on the first day of the week, just after sunrise, they were on their way to the tomb and they asked each other, "Who will roll the stone away from the entrance of the tomb?" But when they looked up, they saw that the stone, which was very large, had been rolled away. As they entered the tomb, they saw a young man dressed in a white robe sitting on the right side, and they were alarmed. "Don't be alarmed," he said. "You are looking for Jesus the Nazarene, who was crucified. He has risen! He is not here. See the place where they laid him. But go, tell his disciples and Peter, 'He is going ahead of you into Galilee. There you will see him, just as he told you.'" (Mark 16:1-7)

Overnight the world changed! On Friday the women had watched Jesus die and then followed along to note where Joseph and Nicodemus buried him. Because of the Sabbath, they could not finish the task of preparing the body for burial. They had hurried to roll the stone in place and then went home and observed the Sabbath. Twenty-four hours later, at sunset on the Sabbath, the women had bought spices to anoint the body, brought them home, and waited for the morning light. They had gone to sleep filled with sorrow, knowing Jesus was dead.

Before dawn the women prepared themselves and their spices and scurried out the door to Joseph's garden. Mary Magdalene and Mary the mother of James must have left before the other women because the gospels say Mary left the house while it was still dark (John 20:1). Perhaps the women had planned to meet the others at the tomb, or perhaps the other women had caught up to them before they arrived at the tomb. Their hearts were still heavy as they walked along the road. They planned to anoint the body of

Jesus in the cool of the day before the heat made the task unbearable.

From a distance the women saw that the stone guarding the tomb was no longer in place. What wild conclusions they must have made at that point. Stunned, surprised, and perhaps panic-stricken, Mary Magdalene may have left the others and run back to Jerusalem to tell Peter and John. She assumed someone had taken Jesus' body. For her, no other explanation was possible. The others cautiously went ahead to investigate. I can imagine them slowly approaching the entrance to the tomb like wary young animals investigating something they had never encountered before. When they approached the dark entrance of the tomb, they hesitantly looked inside.

Jesus was gone! The linen used for his burial was still there, but it no longer covered his body—it lay flat. The body of Jesus was gone. They wondered how. What had happened? What had changed since they had witnessed his burial late Friday? Then two men—actually angels—dressed in gleaming white clothes appeared beside them. Their cautious attitude, which a few moments earlier had changed to wonder, suddenly grew to fear at the presence of these two angels.

One of the angels spoke—perhaps that's why some of the women remembered only one angel instead of two. His words were simple, "Don't be alarmed." Then he gave the reason, "You are looking for Jesus the Nazarene, who was crucified. He has risen! He is not here. See the place where they laid him." Those words announced the most significant change ever heard. Jesus was alive. He was not among the dead any longer.

The words left the women bewildered and stunned. It was too much to believe. In their wildest dreams they would never have imagined such news. No one could! Everyone who heard the news of Jesus' resurrection had to be convinced it was true. During the next 40 days, Jesus would prove that the announcement of the angel was true. At first the disciples would not believe. The women were perhaps afraid to believe such unbelievable news. Jesus was alive!

The resurrection of Jesus changed the sorrow and fear of these women to joy and hope. Even if they did not fully understand it all at the time, everything was different after Easter morning. The world changed for them and for everyone overnight! I'm not exaggerating. The resurrection of Jesus from the dead is an event so significant that it is impossible to exaggerate.

Jesus demonstrated his power over death. Jesus Christ is the only religious leader in the history of the world that has come back to life. All other religious leaders remain dead. They may claim to live on, but they do so only in their teachings and in the lives of their followers. The founders of other religions did not leave their graves behind as Jesus did. Followers of many of these leaders visit shrines where the remains of the leader are kept and revered. Not with Jesus. Disciples of Jesus do not visit his remains in Jerusalem. He is risen!

Every Easter morning my heart is moved to sing, "Hallelujah! Jesus is risen!" Easter morning is very important because it means that all disciples of Jesus will live again. Thank God I am among those with such hope. Like Jesus, we will be laid to rest in graves, but at the word of Jesus we will rise and leave our empty graves behind. Jesus said, "Because I live, you also will live" (John 14:19). No one else can give such victory over death. I treasure this hope. I find comfort in it in good days and bad days. I confront life's challenges, disappointments, and joys with the confidence that I shall rise again as Jesus did. My spiritual journey to Jerusalem always brings me to Joseph's garden. With the eyes of faith I look inside the tomb of Jesus and hear again that it is empty. Praise God! Hallelujah! Death is overcome!

PRAYER: He lives and grants me daily breath;
He lives, and I shall conquer death.
He lives my mansion to prepare;
He lives to bring me safely there.

He lives, all glory to his name!
He lives, my Jesus, still the same.
Oh, the sweet joy this sentence gives:
"I know that my Redeemer lives!" Amen. (CW 152:7,8)

48

Greetings!

So the women hurried away from the tomb, afraid yet filled with joy, and ran to tell his disciples. Suddenly Jesus met them. "Greetings," he said. They came to him, clasped his feet and worshiped him. Then Jesus said to them, "Do not be afraid. Go and tell my brothers to go to Galilee; there they will see me." (Matthew 28:8-10)

Who would believe them? The women had seen the angels and heard the announcement of Christ's resurrection from one of them. Quickly they left the tomb with a strange mixture of joy and fear. They ran to tell the disciples. But would they believe the women?

They had proof, but it was not absolutely convincing. The appearance of the angels confirmed that something unusual had happened. Just as the angels had appeared in the sky above Bethlehem, so the angels had appeared in the empty tomb. In the glow of the morning light, more than one woman had seen the angels. Each one confirmed the incident as a corroborating witness. The linen was neatly in order but did not cover the body of Jesus. Jesus was gone. The stone had been rolled away—something they could not have done by themselves. All these things confirmed their story, but they had not seen or touched the living Jesus.

Then on their way back to Jerusalem, Jesus suddenly appeared before the women. He greeted them and stopped their hurried strides toward the disciples. Jesus gave them one more proof—himself. Perhaps they could not believe their eyes. There he stood before them. But they did not imagine him there; they touched his feet and worshiped him. His body was not still in the grave; their hands touched his feet and no doubt the wounds the nails had made. It was Jesus—the same Jesus who had been crucified. He was alive. The resurrection was a fact beyond doubt in the minds of the women. Jesus had convinced them he was alive.

Stunned and thrilled, they eagerly became his messengers. The angel told them to tell the disciples. Jesus himself told them to tell the disciples. Both Jesus and the angel promised the disciples would see him too. The women had news to tell, so they resumed their run to Jerusalem. They arrived breathless. Between gasps for breath, they told everything they had heard and seen in the light of dawn.

The disciples were amazed at the story the women told. Jesus alive? Was it just the hysterical imagination of the women? Could it be true? In those early morning hours it was too much for them to believe. The story the women told sounded like nonsense. The disciples had not seen Jesus, and it was difficult to believe the exciting story of the women. Despite the raising of Lazarus only a few weeks earlier, the resurrection of Jesus from the dead was too much to believe. They remained unconvinced.

I can understand the reaction of the disciples. When we receive either good news or bad news, we tend to deny it at first. We say, "No, that can't be." On the one hand, this was the greatest news imaginable—Jesus was no longer dead. He arose! It was too much to hope. On the other hand, the disciples feared for their own lives. They hid behind locked doors for fear they might be next. Jesus alive! That meant they no longer needed to fear for their lives because Jesus was more powerful than the threats of the Jewish leaders. It was too much to believe.

My heart may doubt too. As a sinner, I oppose the message of God. My sinful nature finds all kinds of reasons to doubt. I cannot imagine someone coming back to life. I have never seen it happen. Everyone I know who has died has stayed dead. He or she was buried and now rests in the ground. Resurrection from the dead defies all my experience and every principle of medical science. Dead is dead! I've witnessed no exceptions! I can conclude that the story of the women must be hysterical nonsense, just as the disciples did. How could anyone believe such a tale? Besides, the account of the event was written long ago. How can I rely on their ancient record?

Yet I am a disciple of Jesus, and by the work of the Holy Spirit I dare to believe the impossible. I believe that my Savior is powerful.

He can do the impossible. He is true God and is not limited by my intellectual understanding or the evidence of scientific observation. He can do things outside the natural, observable world. The New Testament again and again records his miracles. He did the impossible. He called Lazarus from the dead. He rose from the dead too. I trust him!

Faith doesn't need evidence, only the Word of God. My nature wants to doubt God's Word too. But I also trust Jesus to give me accurate information. He loved me enough to die for me. He will not mislead me to believe something untrue. The words that tell me about him in the Bible are reliable. I trust that Jesus has controlled everything so that I have a clear record of what happened on Easter morning. Why should I doubt what the Bible says? He is risen! The women saw him. They touched him. They believed. I do too.

PRAYER: Dear Jesus, when the world around me wonders how I can believe such nonsense as your resurrection from the dead, draw me back to the message of the women. They saw you and touched you. You rose from the dead. That defies all logic and experience, but help me trust you, your power to do all things, and your love for me. Help me be a messenger of your resurrection even when those I tell do not believe. Your resurrection is too good to keep to myself. Amen.

49

Empty Tomb

Early on the first day of the week, while it was still dark, Mary Magdalene went to the tomb and saw that the stone had been removed from the entrance. So she came running to Simon Peter and the other disciple, the one Jesus loved, and said, "They have taken the Lord out of the tomb, and we don't know where they have put him!" So Peter and the other disciple started for the tomb. Both were running, but the other disciple outran Peter and reached the tomb first. He bent over and looked in at the strips of linen lying there but did not go in. Then Simon Peter, who was behind him, arrived and went into the tomb. He saw the strips of linen lying there, as well as the burial cloth that had been around Jesus' head. The cloth was folded up by itself, separate from the linen. Finally the other disciple, who had reached the tomb first, also went inside. He saw and believed. (They still did not understand from Scripture that Jesus had to rise from the dead.) (John 20:1-9)

From a distance in the first light of the day, the women had seen that the stone no longer covered the entrance to the tomb. While the others went on to investigate the tomb, Mary Magdalene ran to Peter and John. She reported what she thought was the explanation for the open tomb. She simply concluded that the enemies of Jesus had not only crucified him but had taken him out of the tomb and put him where his followers would never find him again. She dashed to tell them the news.

Both Peter and John were together that morning. The other disciples were someplace else. When the mob had arrested Jesus in the garden and led him to Jerusalem, the disciples had forsaken Jesus and disappeared into the darkness. Only Peter and John had followed. They had been together at the high priest's palace—Peter outside, warming himself, and John perhaps inside, watching and listening.

On Friday John had stood at the cross with the women. Peter, however, had kept a low profile after his denial of Jesus, perhaps hiding behind locked doors somewhere in Jerusalem. Mary knew where to find both Peter and John. Out of breath after her dash from the tomb, she pounded on the door. Once inside, she told them her story.

Both Peter and John knew they had to confirm Mary's news. If the tomb was empty, they had to see it for themselves. They had to know whether the body of Jesus had been moved or whether his promise to arise from the dead on the third day was true. Was Mary right? Leaving Mary behind, they both ran toward the tomb. They did not pass the other women. They saw no one who could give them any information about the empty tomb.

John reached the tomb first and stopped at the entrance. He peered inside but did not enter. He caught his breath and waited for Peter. In the growing morning light John saw the strips of linen lying where the body of Jesus was laid on Friday. But no body! The grave was empty!

When Peter came just a few moments later, he did not stop at the entrance but bolted into the tomb to confirm Mary's story. He too saw the strips of linen, but there was more. The burial cloth used to wrap the head of Jesus lay by itself, separate from the linen. Someone had carefully folded it. The body of Jesus was gone! The tomb was empty! But part of Mary's story wasn't accurate. No one had broken into the tomb to remove the body. The linen was still there. Grave robbers would not have unwrapped the body and then moved it. A dead body still needed burial clothes.

John stood stunned for a moment at the entrance, but finally he also entered the tomb. He took a closer look with Peter. He saw too that Mary's story was only partly correct. The body of Jesus was not in the tomb. That was true! But no one had moved it to another location. John believed that Jesus had arisen. He didn't yet understand all the Old Testament prophecies of the resurrection, but he did believe that Jesus had arisen as he had promised. Both Peter and John then went back to their homes. Overnight the world had changed for them too.

I wonder what it was like for Peter and John to stand in the empty tomb. As they looked at the flat linen and the neat napkin, did they remember Lazarus? Jesus had called Lazarus back to life only a few weeks earlier. When Lazarus had obeyed the call of Jesus and appeared at the entrance of the tomb, he had still been wrapped in strips of linen with a cloth around his face. Then Jesus said, "Take off the grave clothes and let him go" (John 11:44). Peter and John found an empty tomb on Easter morning, with the grave clothes lying there. John believed. He found victory in the empty tomb.

I need to stand in this tomb whenever I am troubled by death. Like other Christians, I take the spiritual journey to the empty tomb every Easter. But I find that I need to stand in the empty tomb more frequently as I get older. When age creeps slowly into my joints and shortens my breath, I walk to the tomb of Jesus and discover its victory. It is empty. Jesus has overcome death. He is stronger than death. He no longer needed his grave clothes because he was no longer dead but alive. I find comfort in the face of death nowhere else. Death will take me as it took Jesus, but it cannot hold me anymore than it could hold him. Because I am united with Jesus by faith, I will leave my grave clothes behind too and arise to enjoy the victory he has won for me and all believers.

PRAYER: Lord, when the icy hand of age and death reach for me, bring me to your empty tomb. Age may limit my movement and strength, but I trust in your power. Death may claim my body, but you will command death to loose its grip, and I will arise. Continue to comfort me with the certainty of your empty tomb. Amen.

50

Mary!

Then the disciples went back to their homes, but Mary stood outside the tomb crying. As she wept, she bent over to look into the tomb and saw two angels in white, seated where Jesus' body had been, one at the head and the other at the foot. They asked her, "Woman, why are you crying?" "They have taken my Lord away," she said, "and I don't know where they have put him." At this, she turned around and saw Jesus standing there, but she did not realize that it was Jesus. "Woman," he said, "why are you crying? Who is it you are looking for?" Thinking he was the gardener, she said, "Sir, if you have carried him away, tell me where you have put him, and I will get him." Jesus said to her, "Mary." She turned toward him and cried out in Aramaic, "Rabboni!" (which means Teacher). Jesus said, "Do not hold on to me, for I have not yet returned to the Father. Go instead to my brothers and tell them, 'I am returning to my Father and your Father, to my God and your God.'" Mary Magdalene went to the disciples with the news: "I have seen the Lord!" And she told them that he had said these things to her. (John 20:10-18)

Mary was in no hurry to return to the empty tomb. Peter and John had run to the tomb to confirm her story, but once Mary had told her story, she had no reason to hurry. She believed Jesus was still dead. She assumed someone had moved his body. She had no hope and no joy. She still lived in the sorrow of her Lord's death. The images of the crucifixion and burial on Friday remained locked in her mind. She had not yet found the key to unlock and free them.

As Peter and John ran ahead, Mary slowly walked back to the tomb. They had discovered the empty tomb and left without a word to Mary. Perhaps she had not yet returned to the garden and the tomb. Mary's eyes, blurred by tears, saw nothing. Even when she leaned in to look inside the tomb, she saw nothing. The two angels who reappeared after Peter and John had left even asked, "Woman, why are you crying?" But Mary could only speak out of disappointment, fear, and grief. As quickly as she spoke, she turned away.

Jesus stood before her in that instant and asked the same question the angels had asked. Mary's thoughts had not yet found the key to escape tears and sorrow. Surely the gardener, she thought, must know where they took the body. Jesus' answer was short—one word—"Mary." The familiar voice of Jesus addressed her by name. His greeting called her out of her prison of despair. She turned toward him and blurted out, "Rabboni!" What a surprise! Jesus! Alive! Here! She must have gasped when it all hit her. Her eyes were no longer blurred by tears of sorrow. She saw Jesus alive. He was the key to unlock her thoughts. Finally she was free to soar in hope and joy. The dark prison of grief was only a memory. Life had replaced death.

Mary wanted to hug Jesus and never let him go. Her heart's devotion was based on all she knew of Jesus. She had followed him from Galilee and together with the other women had cared for his needs. She was ready and willing to continue serving Jesus as she had before. But it was not to be. Her relationship with Jesus had to change. He was no longer the Suffering Servant, who humbled himself in order to redeem the world. He was the resurrected Lord, powerful, victorious, and glorious.

Jesus' words stopped Mary from holding on to him as she had before. He was finished with suffering and finished with death. He was alive. The world had been redeemed. In 40 days he would ascend to heaven and rule all things as Savior, Lord, and Victor over death. The work of spreading the news of the resurrection was all that remained to be done. She must go and tell the news to those still trapped in bondage to grief, fear, and death. The disciples, brothers of Jesus, must hear the news. Mary became the Lord's ambassador of life.

What wonderful thoughts came to Mary when Jesus called her by name. He knew her. He still loved her. She was one of his sheep, deeply troubled by sorrow, fear, and doubt. He did not want her to go through the day or the rest of her life with any doubt about his resurrection. He called her to hope and joy with a personal invitation: "Mary!" He was alive. Reassured that Jesus stood before her, her heart jumped for joy.

What wonderful thoughts flood my mind when I hear the personal call of Jesus. He knows my name too. So often I am overcome with the everyday events of life that I am bound in my own thoughts of family troubles and joys, professional ups and downs, or financial advances or setbacks. Then I need to hear the voice of the Good Shepherd call me, "John!" He knows me. He knows my human desire to turn away and stew in my own thoughts and wallow in my own troubles and doubts. I am more inclined to worry than praise. I shed tears of sorrow more readily than I should. I worry more than I turn everything over to the Lord.

My Shepherd calls me and assures me he is alive. Death has been overcome. Yes, what I fear most is really nothing to fear. He is Lord of life. He loves me. He directs me to what is really important. He has work for me to do too. I will renew my effort to share the joy of the empty tomb and make my whole life a song of praise for the victory he has given me.

PRAYER: Lord Jesus, so often I am trapped in my own thoughts of fear, doubt, and sorrow. Sometimes I look at you and your Word and fail to recognize the joy and comfort you provide for me, your fearful, wandering, and worrisome sheep. Break through my sinful tendencies with your gentle invitation to see you as Lord of life. Then fill me with joy that I may share the hope of your resurrection with others. Amen.

51

Grave Robbers?

*There was a violent earthquake, for an angel of the Lord came
down from heaven and, going to the tomb, rolled back the stone
and sat on it. His appearance was like lightning, and his
clothes were white as snow. The guards were so afraid of him
that they shook and became like dead men. While the women
were on their way, some of the guards went into the city and
reported to the chief priests everything that had happened.
When the chief priests had met with the elders and devised a
plan, they gave the soldiers a large sum of money, telling them,
"You are to say, 'His disciples came during the night and stole
him away while we were asleep.' If this report gets to the governor, we will satisfy him and keep you out of trouble." So the
soldiers took the money and did as they were instructed. And
this story has been widely circulated among the Jews to this
very day.* (Matthew 28:2-4,11-15)

Mary's first thought had been the ghoulish idea of grave robbers.
For her it was easier to believe in grave robbers than in the resurrection. The idea that someone had moved the dead body of Jesus
stuck in her head until Jesus himself dispelled it. She had to be convinced that Jesus arose from the grave. All the disciples had to be
convinced. They did not believe Jesus arose at first. They would not
believe it. The idea of the Savior's resurrection was too much to hope
for and too wonderful to believe. It defied the laws of nature as they
understood those laws. Every experience except for three inci-
dents—the youth of Nain, the daughter of Jairus, and Lazarus—
confirmed that the dead remained dead. The empty grave promised
hope, but it was too much for them to believe. So the Savior spent
the next 40 days convincing them he had arisen.

I don't think the soldiers had the same problem. They knew no
one came to steal the body of Jesus. They had been standing guard

when a violent earthquake shook them. They couldn't believe what they saw. The dazzling clothes of an angel blinded them. He was like lightning—bright, sudden, and powerful. The angel rolled back the stone and sat on it; they trembled and passed out. No grave robber could have that effect on seasoned soldiers or, for that matter, on anyone. No, the soldiers didn't believe in grave robbers.

But their story confirmed what the Jewish leaders had said on Saturday. The Pharisees had gone to Pilate, asking for the guard because they wanted to prevent Jesus' disciples from stealing the body and telling people Jesus had arisen. But Jesus had arisen! The angel had come to let the world in on the good news by rolling the stone away. The grave was empty, and the soldiers knew it. They knew grave robbers had not violated the seal on the tomb or carried the body of Jesus out during their watch. The worst fears of the Jewish leaders were confirmed by the report of the guards. Jesus had risen as he said he would.

They could not believe such a thing! The resurrection of Jesus from the dead could not be possible. If Jesus had, in fact, come back to life, it meant all their efforts in the last week were futile efforts defying God. It just could not be! They concluded that they must find a way to discredit the stories of the empty tomb. If they could not disprove the resurrection, they had been fools for opposing Jesus and screaming for his death.

They had to pay the soldiers to report the story of the grave robbers. Rather than accept the simplest explanation—Jesus rose—they continued their strategy of distortion and opposition to Jesus. It was expensive. They paid out a large sum of money to convince the guards to tell the Jewish leaders' version of the resurrection story. But the most expensive part was that they chose not to believe. Their refusal cost them the comfort of victory over death and the hope of eternal life. For them it was easier to believe the lie than the truth.

Men and women still would rather believe almost anything else than believe that Jesus rose from the grave. In our world today people spend millions of dollars to buy books about death and life after death. Sometimes they will travel miles to attend seminars or workshops by religious leaders who do not believe that Jesus arose from the grave. Newspapers, magazines, TV and radio talk shows often discuss the ideas and experiences of those near death or those who claim to have some insight into death and dying. For many it is easier to believe something else—almost anything—rather than believe Jesus rose from the dead. The unbelief of the Pharisees has not disappeared.

Even some Christian churches speak of new life in Christ without believing in the empty tomb. They say the spirit of Jesus lives on in all of us, but they will not confess that the body of Jesus left the tomb on Easter morning. Such an idea is too much for them to believe. They pass off their ideas as the result of scholarship and research. Others claim that the reports of the empty tomb recorded in the Scriptures are nothing more than the hysterical dreams and wishes of the disciples of Jesus. In fact, those who supply different explanations of Easter morning can't believe the resurrection stories any more than the Jewish leaders could.

But Jesus had to convince the disciples. He had to turn Mary away from the natural conclusion her mind had reached. All the disciples had to be convinced that Jesus was alive. It was not their first thought. They only came to believe it after their eyes, ears, and hands convinced them Jesus had arisen. Certainly the resurrection of Jesus from the dead is not the first idea anyone would imagine to explain the empty tomb, but it's the truth. I don't need to search for another explanation.

PRAYER: Lord, so many still cannot believe you rose from the grave. When I read and hear of those who do not believe, draw me to your empty tomb and strengthen my faith in your resurrection. When I doubt or when I am confused by what others say, send your Holy Spirit that I may remain confident that you rose from the dead. Amen.

52

Three on the Road

Now that same day two of them were going to a village called Emmaus, about seven miles from Jerusalem. They were talking with each other about everything that had happened. As they talked and discussed these things with each other, Jesus himself came up and walked along with them; but they were kept from recognizing him. He asked them, "What are you discussing together as you walk along?" They stood still, their faces downcast. One of them, named Cleopas, asked him, "Are you only a visitor to Jerusalem and do not know the things that have happened there in these days?" "What things?" he asked. "About Jesus of Nazareth," they replied. "He was a prophet, powerful in word and deed before God and all the people. The chief priests and our rulers handed him over to be sentenced to death, and they crucified him; but we had hoped that he was the one who was going to redeem Israel. And what is more, it is the third day since all this took place. In addition, some of our women amazed us. They went to the tomb early this morning but didn't find his body. They came and told us that they had seen a vision of angels, who said he was alive. Then some of our companions went to the tomb and found it just as the women had said, but him they did not see." He said to them, "How foolish you are, and how slow of heart to believe all that the prophets have spoken! Did not the Christ have to suffer these things and then enter his glory?" And beginning with Moses and all the Prophets, he explained to them what was said in all the Scriptures concerning himself. (Luke 24:13-27)

The early morning hours had buzzed with reports of the empty tomb. The women had told their story to the disciples. The disciples seem to have gathered together somewhere in Jerusalem to hear the news brought by the women. No doubt the disciples had questioned them over and over again about the details. Mary had told her story too. Peter and John had confirmed that the tomb was just as the women said.

Two men, one named Cleopas, were also among the disciples. The other may have been Luke, but no one knows for sure. The disciples had come to listen to and discuss the events of the day with one another. They had been drawn together by their love for Jesus, and a wonderful bond had developed among them. After the early morning reports, they had heard no new information. The women had seen Jesus, but none of the disciples had. No one could confirm that part of the women's report. Everyone was amazed by what the women had said, but without confirmation no one was ready to believe Jesus was alive.

Sometime on Sunday afternoon, Cleopas and his companion decided to travel to Emmaus. No doubt they had walked up to Jerusalem with Jesus and the others a little more than a week earlier and had seen all that had happened in Jerusalem. Perhaps they had talked themselves out and listened enough. No one reported anything new. After the heat of midday, they had left the others and begun their walk to Emmaus. They didn't hurry. The village was only seven miles away, and they had much to talk about. Along the way they reviewed the details of the past few days and wondered what it all meant.

As they talked with each other, Jesus came up to them as another traveler and walked with them. He listened to their discussion and then joined the discussion with a question. His question stopped them. It surprised them. They had come from Jerusalem, and not only were the disciples interested in these events, but the entire city buzzed with news of the death of Jesus and the early reports of his resurrection. Didn't this man know what everyone was talking about? Their answer to Jesus revealed their sorrow. They loved Jesus; that was clear. They had hoped he would bring redemption, and they knew the promises Jesus made to rise on the third day. It was the third day, but they had no proof except the unconfirmed reports of the women.

Jesus pointed these despondent, weary, and sad disciples to the Scriptures. He taught them an important lesson. The Scriptures provided the spiritual strength, hope, and direction they needed. In a detailed lesson along the road to Emmaus, Jesus explained how the Scriptures predicted each event they were so worried about and even predicted his resurrection. The lesson was not lost on them; their hearts burned within as he spoke to them the truth of the Scripture. When they finally recognized Jesus, they hurried back to Jerusalem to tell all the disciples what they had learned. Jesus was alive.

Days of disappointment and despondency still come to disciples of Jesus. But as Jesus talked with these two disciples, he showed them and us where to go for strength, comfort, and hope—the Scriptures. Jesus won't appear to us as he did on the road to Emmaus, but he does come to us in our daily walks in his Word. If we open his Book and read it, we will find what we need.

Soon the disciples would no longer see Jesus as they had before his crucifixion. But he would not leave them alone and without comfort and strength. The Scriptures tell us about Jesus. When we are in doubt, we can read. The Holy Spirit will work through the Word. When we are confused, we can turn to the truth God has given us in his Word. When our hearts are downcast, like those of the two disciples, Jesus directs us to his Word.

We can still walk with Jesus every day. He desires to walk along with us, listen to our concerns and problems, and then provide what we need to go on. Every time we open the Scriptures, Jesus comes to us. He speaks to our hearts. He is alive. The Scriptures say so.

PRAYER: Lord Jesus, on my daily walk I am often heartsick because of some problem or some difficulty. I need you to walk with me along the road. Direct me to your Word when I am downcast. Work within my heart through that Word so that I may find joy and comfort in your resurrection. Then I will be strengthened to continue on the road you have laid out for me. Amen.

53

Locked Doors

They got up and returned at once to Jerusalem. There they found the Eleven and those with them, assembled together and saying, "It is true! The Lord has risen and has appeared to Simon." Then the two told what had happened on the way, and how Jesus was recognized by them when he broke the bread. While they were still talking about this, Jesus himself stood among them and said to them, "Peace be with you." They were startled and frightened, thinking they saw a ghost. He said to them, "Why are you troubled, and why do doubts rise in your minds? Look at my hands and my feet. It is I myself! Touch me and see; a ghost does not have flesh and bones, as you see I have." When he had said this, he showed them his hands and feet. And while they still did not believe it because of joy and amazement, he asked them, "Do you have anything here to eat?" They gave him a piece of broiled fish, and he took it and ate it in their presence. He said to them, "This is what I told you while I was still with you: Everything must be fulfilled that is written about me in the Law of Moses, the Prophets and the Psalms." (Luke 24:33-44)

Cleopas and the other disciple hurried back to Jerusalem to tell their news and confirm the story the women had told earlier in the day. When they arrived, they discovered that there was new confirmation. Jesus had appeared to Simon sometime during the day. Both reports, the one about Peter and the story of the two from Emmaus, stirred the hearts of the disciples. But it was difficult to put aside their fears. They had gathered in secret behind locked doors. They still feared the Jewish leaders. They still did not believe. It was night, and the lamps flickered, holding the dark outside as they talked about what had happened.

Then suddenly and unexpectedly Jesus appeared among them. Their conversation stopped. They looked at Jesus and then at one another. They doubted their own eyes. Thoughts of surprise, fright, and disbelief flashed through their heads as quickly as lightning streaks from the sky to the ground. Then, as on the stormy Sea of Galilee, Jesus spoke and brought the calm: "Peace be with you." But the calm did not come as quickly to the hearts of the disciples as it did to the waves and wind. They were still startled and frightened.

Jesus rebuked them for their lack of faith. All day they had refused to believe what Mary and the other women had said. When John and Peter had confirmed the reports of the women, the disciples still had not believed. When Peter had told them he had seen Jesus, they stubbornly had refused to believe. In that locked room, the disciples talked about all these reports but always found a way to avoid the truth.

Finally the truth was before them. Jesus was alive. The risen Lord set out to prove that he was alive. First, he showed them his hands and feet. It was the same Jesus who had been crucified. He was not a ghost, a phantom of their imaginations. They touched his hands and feet. But even that did not convince them completely. Fear released its tight grip on their hearts. Then joy and absolute surprise seized them. They could not believe their eyes or their touch.

While they still wondered at what their senses told them, Jesus asked for something to eat. As he took the fish they offered, the truth of the resurrection began to sink into their doubtful hearts. How often had they eaten fish with Jesus! They had spent time together with Jesus in Galilee. They had crisscrossed the Sea of Galilee in the fishing boats of Simon Peter and the others. Jesus had fed the multitudes with bread and fish. Jesus was still Jesus! But he had been crucified and was alive again.

Then Jesus turned these disciples to the Scriptures. As he had explained the Scriptures to the two men on the way to Emmaus, he now opened the Scriptures to these startled disciples. He would soon leave them behind when he ascended. When that happened, they must know where to go for strength and comfort. Jesus pointed them to the Bible. There and only there would they find the truth. Their faith was not to be based on visions and imaginations but on the Scripture.

They finally believed. Jesus was risen. Death could not hold him. As surely as surprise, fright, and disbelief had flashed through their minds, joy, hope, and faith appeared like the sun after a fierce storm. Jesus was alive. Then he left them. They were alone again without Jesus and behind locked doors, this time with joyful and hopeful hearts.

The disciples had reacted to the resurrection of Jesus with understandable skepticism. Like all sinful creatures, they naturally had refused the comfort and hope before them. How often I have been like that. When I look at the sorrows and troubles of life, I am filled with fear and doubt. When I attend the funeral of a friend or relative, my hearts dwells on the sorrow and pain. Sometimes the closer the relationship, the deeper the pain and the more difficult it is to find Jesus and the joy of his resurrection.

But Jesus is as patient with me as he was with the others. He rebukes me too for my stubborn lack of faith. When I wallow in my own pain, I can hear him say, "Why are you troubled, and why do doubts rise in your mind?" As a sinful human, I tend to feel sorry for myself. I look too much at myself and not enough at Jesus. But Jesus raises my vision and points me to the Scripture. In its pages I find Jesus again and the strength, comfort, encouragement, and hope I need.

PRAYER: Lord, when I am overcome by fear, doubt, confusion, and pain, point me to your Word. Help me believe that you are the victor over death even when I feel pain and misery. Do not permit me to base my faith on what I feel inside my heart. Help me base my faith on your Word, no matter what my eyes see or my heart feels. You are risen! Help me find joy in your resurrection even when I hurt. Amen.

54

I Know, Thomas

Now Thomas (called Didymus), one of the Twelve, was not with the disciples when Jesus came. So the other disciples told him, "We have seen the Lord!" But he said to them, "Unless I see the nail marks in his hands and put my finger where the nails were, and put my hand into his side, I will not believe it." A week later his disciples were in the house again, and Thomas was with them. Though the doors were locked, Jesus came and stood among them and said, "Peace be with you!" Then he said to Thomas, "Put your finger here; see my hands. Reach out your hand and put it into my side. Stop doubting and believe." Thomas said to him, "My Lord and my God!" Then Jesus told him, "Because you have seen me, you have believed; blessed are those who have not seen and yet have believed." (John 20:24-29)

The first day of the week came to a close after Jesus had left the disciples alone behind locked doors. He had miraculously appeared in their midst and then left again. The disciples had much to talk about after he left. The stories the women shared with them at the break of day had been confirmed in the darkness at the end of the day.

They all agreed that Jesus was alive. They had all seen him and touched him, and they all finally understood the Scriptures. The written Word had foretold that Jesus would go up to Jerusalem and be handed over to the Gentiles, who would mock, insult, flog, and kill him. But the Word also said he would rise again on the third day. Jesus had taught them the lessons of the Scriptures. They believed and understood.

Only Thomas remained a skeptic. He was not there with the others on Easter Sunday. When he joined them sometime during the following week, the others shared their stories with him. He heard each detail; no doubt he heard each detail more than once. The other disciples did their best to convince him Jesus was alive. Thomas remained unconvinced. He demanded more proof than the words of these men and women. To him it must have seemed like they all had dreamed up this fantastic story together. It just wasn't possible. He wouldn't believe what the Scriptures said either. Thomas must have said over and over again during the week, "Unless I see the nail marks in his hands and put my finger where the nails were, and put my hand into his side, I will not believe it."

One week later the disciples were together again in the house. The doors were locked just as they had been the week before. Perhaps the others had hoped Jesus would return and convince Thomas of the resurrection. Perhaps they had simply decided to gather again to celebrate the Lord's appearance the week before. Did they gather for prayer and encouragement? Whatever the reason, they were together again on Sunday evening.

Suddenly Jesus stood among them as he had done exactly one week earlier. He calmed their hearts with his greeting, "Peace be with you!" Then he turned to Thomas and invited him to touch his wounds. Jesus had heard Thomas during the week. He had watched as the others tried to convince him. Jesus knew the very words Thomas had spoken. When he turned to Thomas, he invited him to look at the nailmarks in his hands and touch the wounds made by the nails. He encouraged Thomas to reach out his hand and put it in the wound left by the spear of the soldier.

What a lesson! Even if Thomas and the others could not see Jesus during the week, Jesus could see them. He had heard their conversations and listened to their words. Some have said Thomas later went to India to share the news about the resurrection of Jesus. I don't know. But wherever he went, I like to think Thomas remembered this lesson. No matter where he went, the Lord was with him. No matter how forsaken or lonely he felt, Jesus heard his words and listened to his prayers. Thomas never had to see Jesus again to know that Jesus would hear his every word and accompany him on every path. Jesus was alive and was the Lord and God of his life.

The lesson of Thomas becomes just as important to me. I have not seen Jesus as Thomas and the others did. I have not talked with them. Yet I believe even though I have not seen Jesus. The Scriptures tell me Jesus died for me and rose again. Jesus has called me to believe and become a disciple. Like Thomas and the other disciples, I believe Jesus sees me even if I do not see him. He hears my conversations and watches me as I walk, drive, sleep, and eat. He knows my troubles, and he listens to my prayers. He is with me every day, just as he promised.

Jesus is the Lord and God of my life too. As my Lord he has purchased me to be his disciple by his holy, precious blood. He loves me. He is Lord and God—all powerful, all knowing, and present everywhere I might go. He has sent me out into the world with the news of his victory over death, just as he has sent all his disciples out into the world to be witnesses. He does not abandon us to the world or leave us on our own to make our way the best we can. He controls all things for our good as he promised. He hears our prayers, and he steps into our personal conflicts, pain, and troubles to give us the strength to go on. Finally, I have his word on it. The Scriptures are his word of comfort and encouragement for me and for all believers of all time. He is Lord and God! Jesus lives and reigns as King of kings and Lord of lords for me and for all believers.

PRAYER: Lord Jesus, I believe. You are my Lord and God. Stand beside me in trouble. Walk with me in sorrow. Guide me with your Word when I am confused. Give me power when I have none. Take me by the hand and lead me where you wish me to go. When my earthly journey is over, welcome me into the paradise you have prepared for me and all believers. Amen.

55

Christ Is Arisen!

Jesus did many other miraculous signs in the presence of his disciples, which are not recorded in this book. But these are written that you may believe that Jesus is the Christ, the Son of God, and that by believing you may have life in his name. (John 20:30,31)

For 40 days Jesus reassured the men and women who followed him that he had arisen. They had to be convinced. Some, like Thomas, took more convincing than others, but Jesus convinced them all that he was alive. The Scriptures record at least 14 appearances of Jesus after he arose. Here is a list:

- Jesus appeared to the women after they saw the angels (Matthew 28:9,10; Luke 24:10).
- Jesus spoke to Mary Magdalene at the tomb (John 20:11-18).
- The two men on the way to Emmaus walked and talked with Jesus; they recognized him when he ate supper with them. One of them was named Cleopas (Luke 24:13-35; Mark 16:12,13).
- At some time during the afternoon of the first day of the week, Jesus appeared to Simon Peter (Luke 24:34; 1 Corinthians 15:5).
- When the ten disciples were together behind locked doors, Jesus appeared to them (John 20:19-24).
- One week later Jesus appeared to the ten again, and this time Thomas was with them (John 20:24-29).
- Jesus prepared breakfast for several of the disciples on the shores of the Sea of Galilee (John 21).
- Paul wrote that Jesus appeared to more than five hundred believers at the same time (1 Corinthians 15:6).

- Paul wrote that Jesus appeared to James (1 Corinthians 15:7).
- Jesus led his disciples out to the vicinity of Bethany and ascended to heaven (Luke 24:50-53).
- Jesus appeared to Stephen just before Stephen was stoned by the Jews in Jerusalem (Acts 7:54-56).
- Jesus appeared to Saul on the road to Damascus (Acts 9:1-8).
- While Saul waited in Damascus, Jesus appeared to Ananias and told him to go to Saul and baptize him (Acts 9:10-22).
- Jesus appeared to John, the disciple he loved, while John was in exile on the Isle of Patmos (Revelation 1:9-20).

The resurrection of Jesus is vital to Christian faith. The apostle Paul put it so clearly: "If Christ has not been raised, your faith is futile; you are still in your sins" (1 Corinthians 15:17). The resurrection of Jesus has been attacked over the centuries. It has been considered a fable, a pious wish, and a lie. Many in our own age do not believe in miracles and cannot accept the miracle of Christ's empty tomb. But he is risen. Because he rose, I will live too and so will you.

I am armed with that hope when I confront sickness, aging, death, and the loss of friends and family. He is risen! No arguments by anyone can change the record God left us in the Scriptures. I may doubt, but even my doubts do not change what the Bible says clearly and without question: the early disciples saw Jesus, and the tomb of Jesus was empty. By the grace of God, I believe what the Bible says even if it defies everything science says and everything my human senses tell me. In Christ *dead* is not *dead*. In Christ we shall all arise from our graves when he returns to claim us as his own.

I'm not alone in my belief either. Thousands, even millions, of disciples have believed in the resurrection of Jesus over the centuries. We all have learned to echo Paul's confidence in the resurrection: " 'Death has been swallowed up in victory. Where, O death, is your victory? Where, O death, is your sting?' The sting of death is sin, and the power of sin is the law. But thanks be to God! He gives us the victory through out Lord Jesus Christ" (1 Corinthians 15:54-57).

PRAYER: Dear Lord Jesus, praise and thanks be to you for the victory over death. Give me the power to claim it as my victory by faith in you, and preserve my faith through all the trials, temptations, and turmoil of this world. Lord Jesus, I pray that you would continue to bring new generations to treasure your suffering and death for the sins of the world and your resurrection from the grave. Amen.

Appendix

The Resurrection of Jesus Christ

A Harmony of the Scriptures
Matthew, Mark, Luke, John, Acts, and 1 Corinthians
(based on the New International Version)

1. The Burial

Now it was the day of Preparation, and the next day was to be a special Sabbath. Because the Jews did not want the bodies left on the crosses during the Sabbath, they asked Pilate to have the legs broken and the bodies taken down. The soldiers therefore came and broke the legs of the first man who had been crucified with Jesus, and then those of the other. But when they came to Jesus and found that he was already dead, they did not break his legs. Instead, one of the soldiers pierced Jesus' side with a spear, bringing a sudden flow of blood and water. The man who saw it has given testimony, and his testimony is true. He knows that he tells the truth, and he testifies so that you also may believe. These things happened so that the scripture would be fulfilled: "Not one of his bones will be broken," and, as another scripture says, "They will look on the one they have pierced."

Later, Joseph of Arimathea asked Pilate for the body of Jesus. Now Joseph was a disciple of Jesus, but secretly because he feared the Jews. With Pilate's permission, he came and took the body away. He was accompanied by Nicodemus, the man who earlier had visited Jesus at night. Nicodemus brought a mixture of myrrh and aloes, about seventy-five pounds. Taking Jesus' body, the two of them wrapped it, with the spices, in strips of linen. This was in accordance with Jewish burial customs. At the place where Jesus was crucified, there was a garden, and in the garden a new tomb, in which no one had ever been laid. Because it was the Jewish day of Preparation and since the tomb was nearby, they laid Jesus there.

2. The Sabbath Guard

The next day, the one after Preparation Day, the chief priests and the Pharisees went to Pilate. "Sir," they said, "we remember that while he was still alive that deceiver said, 'After three days I will rise again.' So give the order for the tomb to be made secure until the third day. Otherwise, his disciples may come and steal the body and tell the people that he has been raised from the dead. This last deception will be worse than the first." "Take a guard," Pilate answered. "Go, make the tomb as secure as you know how." So they went and made the tomb secure by putting a seal on the stone and posting the guard.

When the Sabbath was over, Mary Magdalene, Mary the mother of James, and Salome bought spices so that they might go to anoint Jesus' body.

3. Sunday Morning: The Empty Tomb

After the Sabbath, early on the first day of the week, while it was still dark, Mary Magdalene and the other Mary went to look at the tomb.

There was a violent earthquake, for an angel of the Lord came down from heaven and, going to the tomb, rolled back the stone and sat on it. His appearance was like lightning, and his clothes were white as snow. The guards were so afraid of him that they shook and became like dead men.

While the women were on their way, some of the guards went into the city and reported to the chief priests everything that had happened.

Very early in the morning, the women took the spices they had prepared and went to the tomb. And they asked each other, "Who will roll the stone away from the entrance of the tomb?"

But when they looked up, they saw that the stone, which was very large, had been rolled away. Mary Magdalene, out of whom [Jesus] had driven seven demons, saw that the stone had been removed from the entrance. So she came running to Simon Peter and the other disciple, the one Jesus loved, and said, "They have taken the Lord out of the tomb, and we don't know where they have put him!"

When [the other women] entered, they did not find the body of the Lord Jesus. While they were wondering about this, suddenly two men in clothes that gleamed like lightning stood beside them. In their fright the women bowed down with their faces to the ground, but the men said to them, "Why do you look for the living among the dead? He is not here; he has risen, just as he said. Come and see the place where he lay. Then go quickly and tell his disciples: 'He has risen from the dead and is going ahead of you into Galilee. There you will see him.' Now I have told you. Remember how he told you, while he was still with you in Galilee: 'The Son of Man must be delivered into the hands of sinful men, be crucified and on the third day be raised again.'" Then they remembered his words. So the women hurried away from the tomb, afraid yet filled with joy, and ran to tell his disciples.

4. Peter and John Find the Grave Empty; Jesus Appears to Mary

Peter and the other disciple started for the tomb. Both were running, but the other disciple outran Peter and reached the tomb first. He bent over and looked in at the strips of linen lying there but did not go in. Then Simon Peter, who was behind him, arrived and went into the tomb. He saw the strips of linen lying there, as well as the burial cloth that had been around Jesus' head. The cloth was folded up by itself, separate from the linen. And he went away, wondering to himself what had happened. Finally the other disciple, who had reached the tomb first, also went inside. He saw and believed. (They still did not understand from Scripture that Jesus had to rise from the dead.)

Then the disciples went back to their homes, but Mary stood outside the tomb crying. As she wept, she bent over to look into the tomb and saw two angels in white, seated where Jesus' body had been, one at the head and the other at the foot.

They asked her, "Woman, why are you crying?"

"They have taken my Lord away," she said, "and I don't know where they have put him." At this, she turned around and saw Jesus standing there, but she did not realize that it was Jesus.

"Woman," he said, "why are you crying? Who is it you are looking for?"

Thinking he was the gardener, she said, "Sir, if you have carried him away, tell me where you have put him, and I will get him."

Jesus said to her, "Mary."

She turned toward him and cried out in Aramaic, "Rabboni!" (which means Teacher).

Jesus said, "Do not hold on to me, for I have not yet returned to the Father. Go instead to my brothers and tell them, 'I am returning to my Father and your Father, to my God and your God.' "

Mary Magdalene went to the disciples with the news: "I have seen the Lord!" And she told them that he had said these things to her.

5. Jesus Appears to the Other Women

Suddenly Jesus met [the other women]. "Greetings," he said. They came to him, clasped his feet and worshiped him. Then Jesus said to them, "Do not be afraid. Go and tell my brothers to go to Galilee; there they will see me."

Some of the guards went into the city and reported to the chief priests everything that had happened. When the chief priests had met with the elders and devised a plan, they gave the soldiers a large sum of money, telling them, "You are to say, 'His disciples came during the night and stole him away while we were asleep.' If this report gets to the governor, we will satisfy him and keep you out of trouble." So the soldiers took the money and did as they were instructed. And this story has been widely circulated among the Jews to this very day.

When [the women] came back from the tomb, they told all these things to the Eleven and to all the others who had been with him and who were mourning and weeping. It was Mary Magdalene,

Joanna, Mary the mother of James, and the others with them who told this to the apostles. But they did not believe the women, because their words seemed to them like nonsense.

6. Two Men See Jesus on the Road to Emmaus

Now that same day two of them were going to a village called Emmaus, about seven miles from Jerusalem. They were talking with each other about everything that had happened. As they talked and discussed these things with each other, Jesus himself came up and walked along with them; but they were kept from recognizing him.

He asked them, "What are you discussing together as you walk along?"

They stood still, their faces downcast. One of them, named Cleopas, asked him, "Are you only a visitor to Jerusalem and do not know the things that have happened there in these days?"

"What things?" he asked.

"About Jesus of Nazareth," they replied. "He was a prophet, powerful in word and deed before God and all the people. The chief priests and our rulers handed him over to be sentenced to death, and they crucified him; but we had hoped that he was the one who was going to redeem Israel. And what is more, it is the third day since all this took place. In addition, some of our women amazed us. They went to the tomb early this morning but didn't find his body. They came and told us that they had seen a vision of angels, who said he was alive. Then some of our companions went to the tomb and found it just as the women had said, but him they did not see."

He said to them, "How foolish you are, and how slow of heart to believe all that the prophets have spoken! Did not the Christ have to suffer these things and then enter his glory?" And beginning with Moses and all the Prophets, he explained to them what was said in all the Scriptures concerning himself.

As they approached the village to which they were going, Jesus acted as if he were going farther. But they urged him strongly, "Stay with us, for it is nearly evening; the day is almost over." So he went in to stay with them.

When he was at the table with them, he took bread, gave thanks, broke it and began to give it to them. Then their eyes were opened and they recognized him, and he disappeared from their sight. They asked each other, "Were not our hearts burning within us while he talked with us on the road and opened the Scriptures to us?"

They got up and returned at once to Jerusalem. There they found the Eleven and those with them, assembled together and saying, "It is true! The Lord has risen and has appeared to Simon." Then the two told what had happened on the way, and how Jesus was recognized by them when he broke the bread. But they did not believe them either.

7. Jesus Appears to the Disciples in Jerusalem

While they were still talking about this, with the doors locked for fear of the Jews, Jesus himself stood among them and said to them, "Peace be with you."

They were startled and frightened, thinking they saw a ghost. He rebuked them for their lack of faith and their stubborn refusal to believe those who had seen him after he had risen. He said to them, "Why are you troubled, and why do doubts rise in your minds? Look at my hands and my feet. It is I myself! Touch me and see; a ghost does not have flesh and bones, as you see I have."

When he had said this, he showed them his hands and feet. And while they still did not believe it because of joy and amazement, he asked them, "Do you have anything here to eat?" They gave him a piece of broiled fish, and he took it and ate it in their presence.

Again Jesus said, "Peace be with you! As the Father has sent me, I am sending you." And with that he breathed on them and said, "Receive the Holy Spirit. If you forgive anyone his sins, they are forgiven; if you do not forgive them, they are not forgiven."

Now Thomas (called Didymus), one of the Twelve, was not with the disciples when Jesus came. So the other disciples told him, "We have seen the Lord!"

But he said to them, "Unless I see the nail marks in his hands and put my finger where the nails were, and put my hand into his side, I will not believe it."

A week later his disciples were in the house again, and Thomas was with them. Though the doors were locked, Jesus came and stood among them and said, "Peace be with you!" Then he said to Thomas, "Put your finger here; see my hands. Reach out your hand and put it into my side. Stop doubting and believe."

Thomas said to him, "My Lord and my God!"

Then Jesus told him, "Because you have seen me, you have believed; blessed are those who have not seen and yet have believed."

8. Jesus Appears to His Disciples in Galilee

Afterward Jesus appeared again to his disciples, by the Sea of Tiberias. It happened this way: Simon Peter, Thomas (called Didymus), Nathanael from Cana in Galilee, the sons of Zebedee, and two other disciples were together. "I'm going out to fish," Simon Peter told them, and they said, "We'll go with you." So they went out and got into the boat, but that night they caught nothing.

Early in the morning, Jesus stood on the shore, but the disciples did not realize that it was Jesus.

He called out to them, "Friends, haven't you any fish?"

"No," they answered.

He said, "Throw your net on the right side of the boat and you will find some." When they did, they were unable to haul the net in because of the large number of fish.

Then the disciple whom Jesus loved said to Peter, "It is the Lord!" As soon as Simon Peter heard him say, "It is the Lord," he wrapped his outer garment around him (for he had taken it off) and jumped into the water. The other disciples followed in the boat, towing the net full of fish, for they were not far from shore, about a hundred yards. When they landed, they saw a fire of burning coals there with fish on it, and some bread.

Jesus said to them, "Bring some of the fish you have just caught."

Simon Peter climbed aboard and dragged the net ashore. It was full of large fish, 153, but even with so many the net was not torn. Jesus said to them, "Come and have breakfast." None of the disciples dared ask him, "Who are you?" They knew it was the Lord. Jesus came, took the bread and gave it to them, and did the same with the fish. This was now the third time Jesus appeared to his disciples after he was raised from the dead.

When they had finished eating, Jesus said to Simon Peter, "Simon son of John, do you truly love me more than these?"

"Yes, Lord," he said, "you know that I love you."

Jesus said, "Feed my lambs."

Again Jesus said, "Simon son of John, do you truly love me?"

He answered, "Yes, Lord, you know that I love you."

Jesus said, "Take care of my sheep."

The third time he said to him, "Simon son of John, do you love me?"

Peter was hurt because Jesus asked him the third time, "Do you love me?" He said, "Lord, you know all things; you know that I love you."

Jesus said, "Feed my sheep. I tell you the truth, when you were younger you dressed yourself and went where you wanted; but when you are old you will stretch out your hands, and someone else will dress you and lead you where you do not want to go." Jesus said this to indicate the kind of death by which Peter would glorify God. Then he said to him, "Follow me!"

Peter turned and saw that the disciple whom Jesus loved was following them. (This was the one who had leaned back against Jesus at the supper and had said, "Lord, who is going to betray you?") When Peter saw him, he asked, "Lord, what about him?"

Jesus answered, "If I want him to remain alive until I return, what is that to you? You must follow me."

Because of this, the rumor spread among the brothers that this disciple would not die. But Jesus did not say that he would not die;

he only said, "If I want him to remain alive until I return, what is that to you?"

This is the disciple who testifies to these things and who wrote them down. We know that his testimony is true.

9. The 40 Days and the Ascension

After his suffering, [Jesus] showed himself to these men and gave many convincing proofs that he was alive. He appeared to them over a period of forty days and spoke about the kingdom of God.

He said to them, "This is what I told you while I was still with you: Everything must be fulfilled that is written about me in the Law of Moses, the Prophets and the Psalms." Then he opened their minds so they could understand the Scriptures. He told them, "This is what is written: The Christ will suffer and rise from the dead on the third day, and repentance and forgiveness of sins will be preached in his name to all nations, beginning at Jerusalem. You are witnesses of these things. I am going to send you what my Father has promised; but stay in the city until you have been clothed with power from on high."

On one occasion, while he was eating with them, he gave them this command: "Do not leave Jerusalem, but wait for the gift my Father promised, which you have heard me speak about. For John baptized with water, but in a few days you will be baptized with the Holy Spirit."

So when they met together, they asked him, "Lord, are you at this time going to restore the kingdom to Israel?"

He said to them: "It is not for you to know the times or dates the Father has set by his own authority. But you will receive power when the Holy Spirit comes on you; and you will be my witnesses in Jerusalem, and in all Judea and Samaria, and to the ends of the earth."

Then the eleven disciples went to Galilee, to the mountain where Jesus had told them to go. When they saw him, they worshiped him; but some doubted. Then Jesus came to them and said, "All authority in heaven and on earth has been given to me. Therefore go and make disciples of all nations, baptizing them in the name of the Father and of the Son and of the Holy Spirit, and teaching them to obey every-thing I have commanded you. And surely I am with you always, to the very end of the age. Whoever believes and is baptized will be saved, but whoever does not believe will be condemned."

When he had led them out to the vicinity of Bethany, he lifted up his hands and blessed them. [Then] he was taken up before their very eyes, and a cloud hid him from their sight.

They were looking intently up into the sky as he was going, when suddenly two men dressed in white stood beside them.

"Men of Galilee," they said, "why do you stand here looking into the sky? This same Jesus, who has been taken from you into heaven, will come back in the same way you have seen him go into heaven."

10. The Christian Message: He Is Risen!

Jesus did many other miraculous signs in the presence of his dis-ciples, which are not recorded in this book. If every one of them were written down, I suppose that even the whole world would not have room for the books that would be written. But these are writ-ten that you may believe that Jesus is the Christ, the Son of God, and that by believing you may have life in his name.

Now, brothers, I want to remind you of the gospel I preached to you, which you received and on which you have taken your stand. By this gospel you are saved, if you hold firmly to the word I preached to you. Otherwise, you have believed in vain. For what I received I passed on to you as of first importance: that Christ died for our sins according to the Scriptures, that he was buried, that he was raised on the third day according to the Scriptures, and that he appeared to Peter, and then to the Twelve. After that, he appeared to more than five hundred of the brothers at the same time, most of whom are still living, though some have fallen asleep. Then he appeared to James, then to all the apostles, and last of all he appeared to me also, as to one abnormally born.

For I am the least of the apostles and do not even deserve to be called an apostle, because I persecuted the church of God. But by the grace of God I am what I am, and his grace to me was not without effect. No, I worked harder than all of them—yet not I, but the grace of God that was with me. Whether, then, it was I or they, this is what we preach, and this is what you believed.

But if it is preached that Christ has been raised from the dead, how can some of you say that there is no resurrection of the dead? If there is no resurrection of the dead, then not even Christ has been raised. And if Christ has not been raised, our preaching is useless and so is your faith. More than that, we are then found to be false witnesses about God, for we have testified about God that he raised Christ from the dead. But he did not raise him if in fact the dead are not raised. For if the dead are not raised, then Christ has not been raised either. And if Christ has not been raised, your faith is futile; you are still in your sins. Then those also who have fallen asleep in Christ are lost. If only for this life we have hope in Christ, we are to be pitied more than all men.

But Christ has indeed been raised from the dead, the firstfruits of those who have fallen asleep. For since death came through a man, the resurrection of the dead comes also through a man. For as in Adam all die, so in Christ all will be made alive.